Christmas

Christmas
Decorations · Feasts · Gifts · Traditions

David Baird

MQP

Published by MQ Publications Limited
12 The Ivories, 6–8 Northampton Street
London N1 2HY
Tel: 020 7359 2244
Fax: 020 7359 1616
www.mqpublications.com

ISBN: 1-84072-717-9

1 3 5 7 9 0 8 6 4 2

Printed and bound in China

Contents

Introduction

One of the richest tapestries of life is Christmas—filled as it is with ancient customs and traditions, some even predating the famous birth itself, now woven together with everything we've come to associate with the season since the advent of television and the famous soft drink Santa. But one thing is still certain: those of us who are prepared to give ourselves over to the spirit of Christmas can expect to find love and peace, friendship and forgiveness, kindness, charity, and warmth unlike that at any other time of the year. We feel less compelled by custom and more compelled by generosity to reciprocate in kind.

I have had the pleasure and good fortune to celebrate during the Christmas holidays with people of many varied faiths and beliefs all over the world, atheists and agnostics amongst them. Together we have all managed to get closer to the underlying truth that the world is a better place when we treat each other with kindness, respect, friendship, and brotherly love. Of course a perfectly prepared feast helps too!

Whatever your belief, this book contains a wide array of traditions, expressions, customs, fun suggestions, readings, tips, and treats to help you find or rediscover Christmas. May the paths you choose be peaceful, perfect, and merry.

Make
Christmas
Bright

Get decorating. Start with the entrance to your home and make a welcoming display of greenery, berries, and lights.

Take your friends or family to a Christmas parade or carol concert.

Choose a real tree, preferably one grown for needle longevity, and decorate it with care. Try a Victorian look with candles, ribbons, and wooden toys or mix it up and include some modern baubles.

Make some edible decorations. They're not only pleasing to the eye, but satisfy a few of the other senses, too!

Candy canes represent the staff of the Good Shepherd. The red is his blood and the white is the purity of Christ. Explain this to the children as you hand them out.

Make it a Christmas to remember.

Try to do at least some of these things, and your Christmas will be closer to perfect. And remember there's always next year for what you don't manage.

Design your Christmas to take you well into the New Year.

Decorate the fireplace with lots of greenery. Holly leaves and berries, spare branches from your tree, and some twigs and pine cones make a lovely display.

String popcorn and cranberries together while listening to your favorite Christmas songs.

Create little treasure troves of treats. Fill a bowl with tangerines, chocolate coins, and some walnuts. Add a nightlight and it will glow temptingly.

Don't overdo it with fairy lights, but don't ignore them either. Use inexpensive strings of tiny lights to transform a room. Integrate them into a Christmas wreath, wind them through a garland of natural greenery, or just frame the windows with them.

Take your nearest and dearest on an outing to the country or a Christmas-tree lot and beg or buy—please don't cut for yourself—some broken evergreen branches. Gather them into small, short bundles and wire the bundles to a round framework for the perfect door wreath.

Instead of crashing in front of the television after Christmas dinner, get everyone bundled up warm in sleeping bags and go outside for a little stargazing.

So stick up ivy and the bays, and then restore the heathen ways, green will remind you of the Spring, though this great day denies the thing, and mortifies the earth, and all, but your wild revels, and loose hall.

Henry Vaughan

Get into the Christmas spirit early by going to see the lights being turned on in your nearest city.

Three years after Thomas Edison gave his first public demonstration of electric lights in 1879, his assistant, Edward Johnson, came up with the idea of electric lights for Christmas trees.

Knock, knock.
Who's there?
Mary.
Mary who?
Mary Christmas!

A seasonal tip.
Less equals more:
More calm,
More peace,
More quiet.

As well as observing the Christmas traditions from your childhood, invent some new family traditions of your own.

Fill a flask with hot chocolate and go on an excursion to the beach. You can have a great time beachcombing for driftwood, shells, and pebbles. Use these pieces of "found art" to create your own natural Christmas decorations.

Knock, knock.
Who's there?
Yule.
Yule who?
Yule find out faster if you open the door!

Why go through the turmoil and agony of sorting through strings of damaged old lighting? Invest in some new lights and throw out the old stuff—buying new ones could save your life.

Enjoy using candles around the home, but do remember that you are dealing with a living flame; always place candles on a suitable surface, in a suitable holder, and safely far away from anything that is flammable.

Decorating is always better in pairs—each person can stand back and admire the other's efforts and you'll always have someone to hold the ladder as you stretch to trim the top branches.

Make Christmas truly special by rediscovering old friends and mending broken relationships.

Buy some kazoos and get six, ten, or even more friends together. Make yourselves "Kazoo Carollers" and raise some money for a charity.

In 1895 an American telephonist, Ralph Morris, discovered that strings of lights had already been manufactured to use in telephone switchboards. They gave him the idea of using them on his Christmas tree.

Contact friends and loved ones who are scattered across the globe. Pre-arrange a moment at Christmas when you all light a candle at exactly the same time and think of one another.

Star lights, pin lights, ball lights, flicker lights, lantern lights, fairy lights, frosted bubble lights…there's no excuse not to find seasonal lighting to suit every taste and location, indoors and out. Be creative while being safe.

Try decorating your largest and strongest houseplants with Christmas lights. As with the tree, avoid getting the lights wet when you water and always turn them off before bedtime.

Get your friends together to create a living nativity scene to raise money for charity.

Be careful not to light your interior in such a way that you'll be compelled to watch all your favorite Christmas television shows through flashing reflections from elsewhere in the room.

Can anyone truly hear the word Christmas and not feel even the most minute spark of joy in some corner of their heart?

Make carollers welcome with cookies and hot chocolate or spicy fruit punch. Nothing cuts through the chilly night air like the harmonies of young carollers on your doorstep.

Christmas is the time to let the charity that begins in the home spread out into the wider world.

Snow has a wonderful, magical way of making everything it covers look softer and brighter, cleaner and infinitely more beautiful. If it doesn't arrive, help nature out. Frost some windows and dust the Christmas tree branches with artificial snow.

Make things cosy and read the Christmas story (Matthew 1 and Luke 2:1-20) the night before Christmas.

It costs very little to decorate some candles and everyone is always pleased to receive something lovingly homemade, especially if the gift comes with a tag saying, "May all your Christmases be Bright!"

You cannot please everybody all of the time, so don't try so hard.

Seek harmony.

Organize an office Christmas party that won't end with a job search. Serve punch with only a splash of liquor or wine in it alongside huge platters of tempting—and fairly substantial—food.

Fragrant pomanders are perfect as table or Christmas tree decorations or for scenting rooms, drawers, and cupboards. They also make welcome gifts. They're simple to make; all you need are a few oranges, a pile of cloves, some pins, and a decorative ribbon to hang them with.

Each of us has our notion of our own, unique, ideal Christmas. It's the one we create that reflects our desires and affections, values and traditions.

The best Yuletide decoration is, of course, to be wreathed in smiles. That said, turn your hand to creating a themed evergreen wreath.

What do snowmen eat for breakfast?
Frosted snowflakes!

It was always said of him, that he knew how to keep Christmas well, if any man alive possessed the knowledge. May that be truly said of us, and all of us! And so, as Tiny Tim observed "God Bless Us, Every One!"

Charles Dickens

There's no reason to be concerned about your pint-size Christmas tree. Instead, go for shape and vigor. Remember, little children see all Christmas trees as gigantic and glorious.

Get all your cards out by early December, even to people you barely remember!

Festoon your Christmas tree with popcorn garlands. They make a welcome alternative to tinsel and bestow a snowy effect. All you need is some popping corn, a saucepan, a little oil, a needle, and some sturdy string for threading.

If the spirit takes you, popcorn garlands can be sprayed silver or gold—or any other color that suits your design. But remember, paint makes them inedible!

For colorful, but edible, popcorn garlands, roll the popcorn in diluted food colors before you thread it onto the string.

What message will you be sending to others through your choice of Christmas cards? Why not recycle or create your own?

The way to make a perfect Christmas is not to try to make a perfect Christmas.

Learn something about another country or culture this year by adopting one of their Christmas traditions or preparing one of their special festive dishes.

Make a fig and orange garland for your tree or mantelpiece. You'll need dried figs, oranges that you've sliced and let dry for a few days, and a needle and strong thread. String them in an alternating pattern to make their colors contrast.

Plans get altered, things change, people are unpredictable. Bank on a perfect Christmas and you leave yourself open to frustration and anger.

Always bear in mind what your decorations will say to you and your visitors about Christmas and your feelings toward it.

Rediscover the joy of your childhood Christmases by searching out one of your old Christmas toys and giving it to your children.

These days it's easy to buy everything you need to make homemade Christmas crackers, as they have in England, complete with a snap! Check party stores for the supplies, or go onto the Internet to search for them. Making your own means you can decorate them to your own taste and ensure the quality of the surprise inside as well as the type of jokes they contain.

Listen to some Christmas carols and learn *all* the lyrics— not just those in the first verse.

Bake a simple Yule Log cake and present it to a friend with warm wishes for Christmas.

As we prepare a special Christmas for our nearest and dearest, it's a good time to reflect with gratitude on those who prepared past Christmases for us.

Don't be demoralized by those who describe all the Christmas preparations they've made.

Don't skimp on evergreens such as holly, ivy, and the Christmas tree itself. These symbolize the everlasting life promised to us.

Put your real Christmas tree to good use after you've enjoyed it in the house. Place fruit and birdseed in its branches and take it outside into the bleak midwinter. Not only will it cheer up a depressing winter yard, but birds will also visit to feed and find shelter.

If there is one day of the year that holds the calendar together, it's Christmas Day.

In sixteenth-century Germany, Martin Luther is said to have brought a tree indoors and decorated it with candles to show the children what stars looked like at night in the forest.

Decorate a special log to set alight on Christmas Eve and keep that Yule log blazing in your open fire. It's considered bad luck to light a fresh fire during the Twelve Days of Christmas, so keep at least an ember glowing all the time.

Make some colorful paper chains with children, and as you contemplate the links, let them represent your links to others celebrating Christmas around the world.

How do you know if a reindeer has been in your refrigerator? Look to see if there are any hoof prints in the butter dish!

Consider wrapping your gifts as a pleasure, not a chore, and make them as attractive as possible using ribbons, bows, and homemade tags.

Buy some cheap Christmas baubles of various sizes and use hot glue to embellish them by adding natural objects or bright costume gems.

No one deserves a narrow-minded, dull, or petty Christmas. Try to make Christmas the time to recover the things that really matter: family togetherness, community, faith, and fun.

The true spirit of Christmas is love. Let this feeling shine through your decorations.

We all want the holidays to go smoothly, but they rarely do. Share your Christmas catastrophes with others and you won't feel so alone.

Christmas joy is the joy of brightening other people's dark lives.

Go outside for a walk in the crisp winter sunshine on Christmas Day and look out for gleeful children having fun on their new Christmas bikes.

The human traditions of Christmas are not holy commandments. If God was against our partying, He would never have turned the water into wine.

You can make an unusual and inspired Christmas decoration by filling an old pair of woollen mittens with potpourri. Tie the mittons together with ribbon in a seasonal color and hang the decoration in a doorway or somewhere it can be smelled when you pass by.

"Dick! Now I cannot—really, I cannot allow any dancing at all till Christmas Day is out," said old William emphatically. "When the clock ha' done striking twelve, dance as much as ye like."

Thomas Hardy

Christmas should never be treated with indifference. That is as certain to destroy it as bigotry would.

Set up a tabletop crib in your home and each day watch the drama unfold as you move the Three Wise Men closer to it—until, at last, they arrive on Twelfth Night.

Buy some gold leaf from an artist's supply store and gild some walnuts and candy canes for decoration.

Who beats his chest and swings from Christmas cake to Christmas cake?
Tarzipan!

Read a classic Christmas book, such as Charles Dickens's *A Christmas Carol* or *How The Grinch Stole Christmas* by Dr. Seuss.

Get busy making some holiday cushions in medieval or contemporary designs to scatter invitingly around the home.

If you are desperate for a white Christmas, then guarantee it by traveling to snow-country for your Christmas holidays.

Christmas has a curious way of putting us into a state of suspended animation for its duration. Most people are snapped back into reality only with the arrival of the January bank statement.

Let your home become the stage for merriment during the festive season.

Brush up your skill at making hot chocolate—you're going to need it!

'Twas Christmas broach'd the mightiest ale;
'Twas Christmas told the merriest tale;
A Christmas gambol oft could cheer
The poor man's heart through half the year.

Sir Walter Scott

Many a defeated, empty heart has been filled by the sound of a carol.

What activity is most meaningful to you? What would make the season more fulfilling and joyful? Make sure to include it in your plans.

Everybody needs a sense of humor to cope with the Christmas holidays. Spend a day making up Christmas jokes and inventing fun new family games.

Believe me, there are people who feel fine about getting into the Christmas spirit by watching people being helped by others while offering no help themselves. Make sure you're not one of them.

If "if's" and "but's" were candy and nuts, wouldn't it be a merry Christmas?

Arm yourself with treats and bonbons to defuse potential flare-ups from the younger ranks. As George Bernard Shaw observed, "What use are cartridges in battle? I always carry chocolate instead."

Mom, can I have a dog for Christmas?
No, you can have turkey like everyone else!

Who better to offer a suggestion of what to fill a Christmas stocking with than author Roald Dahl? As he said, "Never mind about 1066, William the Conqueror, or 1087, William the Second. Such things are not going to affect one's life…but 1932, the Mars Bar, 1936, Maltesers, and 1937, the KitKat—these dates are milestones in history and should be seared into the memory of every child in the country."

What do Eskimos use to hold their homes together?
Ig-glue!

Stocking fillers are something you can collect all year round. Find a little bit of Christmas at any point of your year by dedicating some of your lunch breaks to searching for some special Santa treats.

Before you begin your Christmas preparations, you should mentally define the Christmas that you seek.

First, you must ask yourself what Christmas means to you and single out everything that's important to you at Christmas time.

"If it happens, fine. If it doesn't, we'll get by"—that's a good motto to have at this time of year.

Be careful that you, the children, or the pets don't eat any of your tree's inedible Christmas decorations... Someone may get tinsel-itus!

Take a moment to remember.

Everybody gets a little stressed at Christmas, but stressed is only the word desserts spelled backwards—so whenever it hits, invent a new Yuletide dessert.

Arguments for a natural tree:
A natural Christmas tree is biodegradable—the trunk and branches can be used as a mulch for gardens and parks. Mulches make a protective barrier for the roots of other plants and vegetation, prevent weed growth, retain moisture, and provide vital nutrients as they slowly decompose.

Perfect needn't mean pressure. By defining what you want in a Christmas celebration, you'll also be able to realize what's realistic and achievable—and what's not.

Sumptuous decorations and brilliant entertainments may not be what you are seeking. You might prefer to spend a quiet time with friends and loved ones, sitting by the fireside with a mug of hot chocolate and the gentle sound of carols in the background.

Arguments for a natural tree:
Every year, millions of Christmas trees are grown to cope with the holiday demand—think of all that extra oxygen they give out that wouldn't exist if we all switched to artificial trees.

Compiling a card list is a good reason to sit down and relax into the Christmas spirit.

If you could have Christmas any way you wanted, how would it be? What are its flavors? Its aromas? How would your ideal Christmas look and feel?

Christmas is often a time when we forget that we have choices and end up going along with what others want. If you don't make your own choices, you may be left feeling disappointed.

Include something in your Christmas plans that will transport you back to your happy childhood feelings and memories.

Invest in an Advent calendar that you can use every year, with small compartments to hold candies and tiny toys—each morning you'll look forward to opening a window.

In late November, spend a day with your children making your own candies and cookies using cookie cutters shaped like trees, snowmen, angels, and reindeer. Then place them inside the compartments of your calendar.

Only when you are true to yourself at Christmas can you hope to spread peace and goodwill to others.

Never base your Christmas on the expectations other people may have of you. Make your own decisions and stick to them.

Some people make Christmas far more complicated and expensive than it needs to be. Many a Christmas is ruined when the people preparing it are too tired, broke, or stressed out to enjoy it.

The joy of Christmas is in sharing each other's burdens. When it comes to preparations, don't try to go it alone.

Perhaps if we allowed ourselves to remember the warm glow of our childhood Christmases we would not be—at the very mention of the word—so haunted by the unending list of preparations for it.

Christmas didn't begin in the mall,it began in the heart of God, and it can only be perfect when it reaches the heart of man.

Remember to stock up on batteries to cope with the demands of decorations, toys, remote controls, and alarm clocks!

Make your home a winter wonderland of tender gazes, meaningful kisses, loving hugs, kind thoughts, and warm hearts. What can compare with the special joy these bring?

Tempers can become a little frayed at Christmas. Outside, carollers sing about peace on earth, but unfortunately they don't mention your family room.

Arguments for a natural tree:
Christmas trees are often planted on otherwise barren slopes or under power lines where no other crops will grow—making a great improvement to the landscape.

A kissing-bough was often hung from the ceiling in olden times. It consisted of a round ball of twigs and greenery, decorated with seasonal fruit. It was the precursor to the bunch of mistletoe, under which no lady could refuse a kiss. Why not make one for the hallway?

Arguments for a natural tree:
For every natural Christmas tree cut, two or three seedlings are planted, ensuring continued environmental benefits and a plentiful supply.

Be well prepared with a contingency plan to cope with any surprises and disasters that may come your way. Christmas is a time that challenges us all creatively and certain projects will inevitably defeat us, but don't let that make you feel disheartened.

Don't just sit in front of the television after Christmas lunch—get all the family together and play charades, cards, or a family board game.

To serve is beautiful, but only if it is done with joy, one's whole heart, and a free mind.

Mull some wine or brew some tea, lay out a plate of homemade cookies, and dedicate a restful day to savoring them.

Arguments for a natural tree:
Imagine how many landfill sites it would take to dispose of all the artificial trees in the world used at just one Christmas....

Let your Christmas be filled with things that are truly good. Take comfort in your relationships with others and seek warmth from love and friendship. Give your strength to those who need help and try to develop the humility to accept help from others.

Christmas is the launching pad for the New Year to come. Resolve to go forward in peace and with a willing heart, for nothing is impossible.

Make a festive door-knocker. Christmas doesn't knock— you knock and Christmas invites you in.

A new year unfolds like a blossom on the tree of life. Create a new feeling to acknowledge its arrival.

Christmas Eve is the perfect time to watch a classic Christmas movie, such as *It's A Wonderful Life*, while you are making your final preparations for the big day.

If you plan to make Christmas gifts, give yourself enough time. Each Christmas leaves in its wake a sea of ill-fitting cardigans and half-finished projects.

The argument for real Christmas trees is compelling when you consider their environmental benefits. Not only do they serve as a natural wildlife habitat, they increase soil stability and provide a valuable improvement to the land.

Take time out to relax by the fire. Create an atmosphere and read "The Night Before Christmas." If you don't have children to read it to, read it for yourself.

List which Christmas activities usually cause you the most stress and greatest anxiety, then take pains to ensure that these spoilers do not crop up again this year.

Every year at this time, someone, somewhere is dreaming of a white Christmas "…just like the ones I used to know."

A Time
for Giving

No other time of the year is so stressful and yet so exciting.

We run around, where angels fear to tread, composing list after list of cards to buy, gifts to track down, decorations to put up, and food to prepare, fueled by an ever-glowing ember of some Christmas past— a childhood memory that warms our hearts all the way from the nursery to the grave.

Gifts don't need to be expensive; I was once handed a package of instant soup mix by a somewhat-broke actor with a simple homemade, seasonal label wishing me a "Souper Christmas!"

Give a loaf of bread—to friends who were there when you really "kneaded" them!

Turn up at the door with a big bunch of holly, a loving smile and the greeting, "Happy holly days!"

Mix up a seasonal potpourri and give it to a friend with the wish that its scent brings thoughts of special Christmases past.

Give a buddy a decorated bag of nuts with a tag that simply proclaims, "I'm nuts about you!"

Present a pal with a set of measuring spoons with a tag declaring, "I wish you joy beyond all measure!"

Turn your skills to a friend's advantage—offer a certificate awarding a day of curtain-making, gardening, plumbing, or driving.

Why not give a big bunch of bananas tied with a bow: "Merry Christmas— To the Best of the Bunch!"

Unless you are absolutely "with it," it's better to give a teenager cash or a gift certificate to a media store than to come home with the wrong CD.

To your enemy, offer the gift of forgiveness.

To an opponent, offer the gift of tolerance.

To a friend, offer the gift of your heart.

To all about you, offer the gift of charity.

To each child, offer the gift of your own good example.

To yourself, offer the gift of self-respect.

The best of all gifts under any Christmas tree is that of giving each other a happy and peaceful Christmas.

With every bit of love, and every gift we give, no matter what the time of the year—if it comes from the heart, then it's Christmas cheer.

Christmas is about filling empty hearts with the most generous of all the gifts you can give—friendship.

Gifts, believe me, captivate both men and Gods. Jupiter himself was won over and appeased by gifts.

Ovid

Let your Christmas lights be the light of your love and celebrate Christmas by giving the gift of that light to those who need it most.

Write a lovely poem or search for one that says it all, then present it in a frame with a photograph to someone you adore.

Humble hearts receive the greatest gifts at Christmas.

Forget my past, but remember my present!

Let the joy that you give to others be the joy that comes back to you. A festive gift is always given in a joyous or loving way.

Collect attractive, inexpensive costume jewelry from thrift stores and antiques stores. Polish your presents and set them in a special jewelery box—this is an ideal gift for a girl in her early teens.

As you shop, reflect a moment upon why you are giving gifts. Is the motivation one of love for the intended recipient?

Give someone an experience of a lifetime. Book them a flying lesson, a spin in a racing car, a hot air balloon trip—there's something amazing for everyone.

Give a close friend the gift of a special night out at the wonderful Christmas ballet, *The Nutcracker*.

Give the gift of a friendly smile to your fellow shoppers.

Consider the gifts we receive from others. Do we deserve them? In the story of Christmas, God illustrated his love by giving the greatest gift of all to mankind—an infant named Jesus.

We give and receive presents in honor of the gift God gave to us.

Christmas teaches us that the greatest gift to receive is love, and the greatest gift we give to another is the devotion of our heart, mind, and soul.

May peace be your gift at Christmas and your blessing all year through.

If you dread the annual trawl around stores in search of presents, change all that. Light a fire, pour yourself a glass of wine, and go online! Internet shopping can be fun and is often less expensive. You can compare prices and, provided you don't leave it too late, everything will arrive by the big day.

Presents, I often say, endear absents.
                                    Charles Lamb

Wrap a couple of stand-by presents—a box of chocolates, a bottle of wine, or a book—and slide them under the Christmas tree for the unexpected guest or the person you forgot. Make it something you would like to receive under those circumstances as well as something you could use yourself if you don't need to give it after all.

If you have a hobby such as cross-stitching or watercolor painting, don't be too bashful to give your handiwork to a friend or relative as a gift.

No matter who visits at Christmas, a little imagination leads you to a suitable gift. For example, if a fisherman turns up, give him some cas-ta-nets!

We can all relive our most precious childhood Christmas moments through our own children or by providing a similar special moment or gift for a friend's or relative's child and hearing all about their reaction.

Never leave things to the last minute. You can shop for gifts at any time of the year—in fact, the January sales are a good place to start. Why not wrap some Christmas presents on a rainy summer's day?

If you buy battery-operated goods as gifts, have the foresight to also include rechargable batteries—they're so much better for our environment.

The exchange of Christmas presents ought to be reciprocal, not retaliatory.

If we were capable of putting our love for others into words and actions, then we could avoid the annual stampede through the malls to buy presents that attempt to do it for us.

Christmas is a time for each of us to be as charitable as our means will allow—even if the best you can offer is to give someone your blessing.

The least fattening and most memorable feast you could give to anyone at Christmas is a good book.

If you spend money to give people joy, that is not being commercial.

Each year, Christmas becomes a race to see which gives out first—your money or your goodwill.

If the budget is tight this year, invite your friends and family to visit after Boxing Day—the day after Christmas. You'll be able to buy their gifts at the post-Christmas sales.

Write a recipe for home-baked bread on some elegant note cards and bake some small, delicious loaves. Put the bread and cards into festive bags and deliver the loaves on the day you bake them.

Purchase not friends by gifts; when thou ceasest to give, such will cease to love.

Thomas Fuller

To a friend or loved one, if you are with them at Christmas, that's the greatest gift.

Write out a beautifully handwritten recipe card for a simple seasonal dish and put it in a small gift basket or a decorated box with all the necessary ingredients.

If you have a computer, compile and design a friend's family tree. Print and frame it for them.

Happy, happy Christmas, that can win us back to the delusions of our childhood days, recall to the old man the pleasures of his youth, and transport the traveler back to his own fireside and quiet home!

Charles Dickens

Candles are easy to find and relatively inexpensive. Buy lots and tie them in small bundles with rustic-looking twine or satin ribbon. Include cinnamon sticks for fragrance and attach a handwritten tag.

Hobby wreaths are fun to create and a joy to receive. Make an ordinary Christmas wreath but add a few items that relate to your friend's favorite pastime— a golf ball, some tees, and a miniature bottle of whiskey, for example.

In a flea market, thrift store, or antiques store, find a pretty orphaned saucer, plate, or bowl and fill it with your friend's favorite sweets, nuts, or chocolates. Cover with plastic wrap and add a gift tag.

Buy a friend several small bags of different fresh ground coffees and a nice big mug—just the thing for Christmas morning.

Don't panic if you've missed the date to mail overseas packages. Go online and send mail-order gifts—the chances are that they'll arrive on time and you can breathe a huge sigh of relief.

Collect old cookie and cake tins or decorated boxes all year long. As Christmas approaches, start baking! A tin of homemade cookies or fruit cake is always a treasured gift.

Buy some movie tickets for yourself and a friend and deliver them attached to a box of popcorn.

An earthenware pot filled with bulbs or seed packets pleases any gardener.

When money is an issue, plan ahead. A few pennies a week soon add up to something significant, so put aside whatever you can throughout the year. When Christmas arrives, make a budget and stick to it. Present your gifts beautifully and with all your love—that will double their value.

Make some personalized stationery for a grandparent, great aunt or elderly friend: make beautifully designed letterhead paper and notes for them. Find a lovely box, add a pen, and wrap them in homemade gift wrap for a finishing touch.

A few aromatic oils or aromatherapy candles make a fragrant gift—present them as you would like to receive them.

Catch friends and family on camera throughout the year at happy moments or special places, then give them a snapshot in an unusual frame or put several photos in a small attractive album.

Get some Christmas cookie cutters and bake lots of cookies. Arrange them in a box or basket, or on a plate, add a hand-written recipe card, and deliver!

Keep your eye out for distinctive boxes and baskets all through the year—they'll come into their own for putting special presents for friends and family in at Christmas time.

Fill a small basket with several tastes from a specific country: maybe some bottled vine leaves, a jar of olives, some halva, and feta cheese. Add a Greek seasonal greeting: *"Kala Christouyenna!"*

Get gardening. If you've got a greenhouse or a spare windowsill, buy some small pots and plant some young fir trees. When Christmas comes, add a few homemade decorations—edible ones are good—and a red ribbon and present them!

Rich gifts wax poor when givers prove unkind.

William Shakespeare

Give a pie pan, complete with ingredients and a recipe card.

Make your own Chinese-style fortune cookies and put fortunes written specially for the recipient inside them. Offer them in a sealed jar.

Scour thrift stores, antiques stores, and flea markets for nice big glasses, glass vases, or glass jugs. Wash them until they gleam, then fill them halfway up with potpourri. Decorate a hand-made tag, perhaps with a dried rose petal from the potpourri, and tie it on.

You can find single bone china cups and saucers in thrift and antiques stores at very reasonable prices. One of these and a pound of special tea make an excellent gift for someone living on their own.

Give the gifts of your patience, respect, and understanding to busy and tired sales assistants at this hectic time of year.

Scan shelves throughout the year for bin ends and orphan bottles of wine from small wineries and put them aside as gifts for Christmas.

Get creative and make your own unique wrapping paper from florist's paper or newsprint decorated with festive ink stamps.

Spoil the oldest members of the family with mugs of hot cocoa and get them to tell you their memories of Christmases past.

Make your own seasonal potpourri from broken cinnamon sticks, dried orange and lemon peels, whole cloves, nutmeg shavings, pine cuttings, and cypress essential oil.

Think ahead! Buy some very young inexpensive bonsai trees and nurture them for a couple of years. Then present them with a snippet of Eastern wisdom to a deserving friend.

For someone elderly, mix up a selection of old-fashioned sweets to remind them of their childhood. Rootbeer balls, licorice sticks, peppermints, and butterscotch nuggets are good to start with.

If you have a friend who is in hospital or who can't get out and about because of sickness, get a small Christmas tree and decorate it. Choose miniature toys and festive candies for a child; cookies, cinnamon sticks, and pomanders for an adult.

Pass on your unwanted Christmas gifts to charity stores, your local hospital, or a nearby school—let others enjoy making use of the things you don't need.

Give the gift of time. Write a note to a loved one promising a Saturday a month devoted to doing whatever they would like to do with you—go for a picnic, see a movie, or even clean out the garage.

Find some unusual bottles and decant wine or cider vinegar into them. You could also fill small jars with herbs, spices, or your own homemade pickles or jams.

If you can afford to buy a toy or two for a needy child or a family going through hard times, deliver your gift anonymously.

Some places become very cold at Christmas. There are many uprooted people and refugees who would be grateful to receive your used coats and jackets. Ask at your local church or community center to find out the best way to donate to them.

Dedicate a day to helping an elderly relative or neighbor get ready for their Christmas. Help brighten their surroundings and bring some Christmas cheer into their lives.

When we discover that the joy we give to others is joy given back to us, then we have discovered the true Christmas spirit.

We take the Christmas glitter and glamor for granted when we have our own car, but perhaps an elderly neighbor doesn't have such easy access to these delights. Give them a gift of a special outing.

Christmas is a time for giving. Pass on the charitable feeling as a gift to a friend by making a donation in their name to a worthy cause close to their heart.

Christmas would be happier still if we could keep the gifts we give to others and give them the ones they give to us.

Make your Christmas spending plan and stick to it. When you have a plan, you have an effective layer of armor against outside pressure to overspend.

Don't allow your emotions to force your purse to open. There's nothing advertisers want more than to prick your conscience just enough to get money out of you.

The more you spend in blessing the poor and lonely at Christmas time, the happier your heart.

For some, all they want for Christmas is the day after it!

One of the nicest things about Christmas is that you can make people forget a bad past with a good present.

Stay within your budget. Christmas loses all meaning when you place your loved ones in jeopardy for the sake of just one day.

Preserving jars are very affordable. Gather as many as you need, then pickle your own vegetables and make some fruit jams. Add festive labels and cover the lids with a circle of gingham or fabric with a Christmas motif. Tie on the covers with colored string or yarn.

Christmas awakens in each of us great joy, which we express creatively with tinsel and lights.

In suggesting gifts: Money is appropriate, and one size fits all.

William Randolph Hearst

Most people want more of the intangible traditions of the season—companionship, music, spiritual reflection, and love. But we're so obsessed with the Christmas gift tally that we wind up with stress, hassles, and shopper's burnout.

Have a more meaningful and satisfying holiday by spending less money on it. Instead, substitute far more satisfying gifts such as homemade presents and time spent together.

Roll up a pile of comic books and tie them with a bow.

Always keep an eye open for appealing secondhand books.

Make a promise to someone to be there when you are needed.

Look for interesting but inexpensive items from different countries in charity shops or on the Internet.

One good gift is worth lots of little trifles together. Go for quality, not quantity. Remember, the Magi each brought the infant Jesus one gift.

We may here say that Christmas gifts, worked by the giver, are always more cherished than those which are purchased; and for a very natural reason.
Peterson's Magazine, December 1860

"At this festive season of the year, Mr Scrooge," said the gentleman, taking up a pen, "it is more than usually desirable that we should make some slight provision for the poor and destitute, who suffer greatly at the present time. ...We choose this time, because it is a time, of all others, when Want is keenly felt, and Abundance rejoices."

Charles Dickens

The Many Faces of St. Nicholas

He exists as certainly as love and generosity and devotion exist, and you know that they abound and give to your life its highest beauty and joy. Alas! How dreary would be the world if there were no Santa Claus!

Editor, *The New York Sun*

Ask a child if he or she believes that Santa Claus exists and most say they do. Of course it's disputed whether there is such a person or thing as Santa Claus, but as adults the level of belief depends on the extent that we understand the Santa Claus story.

St. Nicholas was a real person.

St. Nicholas is the patron saint of more causes than any other saint.

Patron saints have lived lives that are worthy examples of how to follow Jesus Christ faithfully and, as part of the communion of saints, they intercede on behalf of all those who call upon them.

St. Nicholas is most famous for being the patron saint of children, and there are several tales of his rescuing them from danger and restoring them to their loving families.

Less known perhaps, is that St. Nicholas is the protector of ships and sailors who look to him to provide safe passage and protection from storms.

According to one legend, Nicholas was sailing incognito to the Holy Land when he dreamed of danger. He warned the crew of an impending storm and reassured them that God would protect them, but when the storm hit, one of the crew was killed when he fell from the rigging. There was great relief when the storm subsided, but even more so when Nicholas prayed for the fallen sailor and he miraculously rose from the dead. As Bishop of Myra, Nicholas's concern for the welfare of his people and his rock-solid belief earned him widespread respect and popularity as a model for all bishops.

Children all around the world know and love St. Nicholas. He may be known by different names and look quite different, depending on where you encounter him, but it's the same St. Nicholas.

Nicholas, always alert to the needs of others, gave in secret, expecting nothing for himself in return. His selfless acts of kindness and generosity led to his being beatified as a saint.

For centuries, St. Nicholas's tomb in Myra was a popular pilgrimage site as reverence for the saint grew and spread throughout the Christian world.

St. Nicholas taught the Gospel simply so that ordinary people could understand it, and he lived out his faith and devotion to God by helping the poor and all in need.

The most famous legend concerning St. Nicholas tells of how he saved the three daughters of a destitute man from prostitution by anonymously leaving three bags of gold coins on their window ledge at night.

A French story tells of three small children who were killed by a butcher when they sought shelter in his store being brought back to life when St. Nicholas suddenly appeared and said a prayer over them.

Stories of St. Nicholas's kind acts and his compassion toward children are told all over the world, and often they are the same legends. St. Nicholas's example still inspires acts of charity and generosity.

Nicholas, a young man of good faith and deed, was brought into the church and consecrated as the new Bishop of Myra: "Nicholas, servant and friend of God, for your holiness you shall be bishop of this place."

In 325, at a council of bishops from all over the world, Nicholas slapped Bishop Arias from Egypt when he insisted that the Son Jesus was not equal to God the Father. Nicholas was stripped of his office and imprisoned. In prison that night, Jesus and Mary visited him and returned his bishop's stole and his book of the Gospels. When Nicholas was discovered, fully garbed and reading the Gospels in his locked cell, he was immediately reinstated to his position of Bishop.

Legend has it that Nicholas was chosen as Bishop of Myra in a very mysterious way. While praying, the senior Bishop heard a voice telling him that if the first person to enter the church the next morning was named "Nicholas," he was to be the new Bishop. The next day, the Bishop waited at the doors. A young man arrived and said, "I am Nicholas."

A man of convictions, Nicholas was by no means timid and he was always doing what was necessary for his people and to protect the Christian faith.

St. Nicholas is also the patron saint of the wrongly accused and wrongly condemned, and many tales recount his saving the innocent at the last moment.

One legend tells how Nicholas ran to the aid of three innocent men who were about to be unjustly beheaded. He fearlessly disarmed the executioner, freed the men, and set about proving their innocence.

While he was still a boy, Nicholas's parents died, but even at such a young age his generosity, piety, and selflessness were clearly evident. He obeyed Jesus's words to the rich man— "sell what you own and give the money to the poor"—and used his whole inheritance to assist the needy.

Bishop Nicholas pleaded with Emperor Constantine to relieve the Myran people of the taxes that caused them so much suffering. The Emperor signed a document agreeing to this, but his finance ministers tried to change his mind. Before they could, Nicholas threw the document into the sea and it washed ashore in Myra where it was put into action.

St. Nicholas has been chosen as the special protector or guardian of a great many classes of people, cities, churches, and even countries.

The stories of St. Nicholas often have a universal theme. They tell of children forcibly taken from their families to everyone's great grief and despair, and then the miracle of their return.

In Greece returning sailors show their gratitude to St. Nicholas by putting up silver and wooden icons of their ships in their home port.

Don't be surprised to hear sailors in some parts of the world saying, "May St. Nicholas hold the tiller" instead of "Bon voyage."

When a ship was caught by a storm in the eastern Mediterranean Sea, the sailors cried to Nicholas for help. He appeared to them in a vision and saved them. Later, the sailors went to give thanks at a church in Myra and they met Nicholas in person. He told them that a life devoted to God makes a person so clear-sighted that he can see others in danger and hear their calls for help.

The many famous stories about his life show an effective and resourceful Nicholas helping his people in times of need—in ways both normal and miraculous—during his life, and even after his death.

Icons in many Eastern churches show Jesus returning the Gospels to St. Nicholas and Mary bringing him his bishop's stole.

Emperor Constantine is said to have had a dream in which he was told to free three men who were to be executed. When he asked the figure in his dream who was bringing the message, he was told, "Nicholas, Bishop of Myra; God has sent me to tell you to free these men."

The symbol for St. Nicholas is three gold balls because the tale of the gold coins is sometimes told with gold balls replacing the bags of coins.

St. Nicholas lived his life in devotion to Christ, he loved children, and he cared for the needy by bringing them the love and healing of Christ. We can honor St. Nicholas by following his example of selfless giving.

One miraculous tale tells that when famine struck Myra, Bishop Nicholas implored the sailors of ships carrying cargoes of wheat to Alexandria to give a measure of grain from each ship so that his people would survive. He promised them that they would not reach their destination with a short load, so the sailors gave him a good measure of wheat to save the starving people. And indeed when the ships were unloaded at Alexandria they all still contained their full cargo of grain.

It is said that Nicholas saw the angels come to take him to heaven when he died. As they came to collect him, he began to recite the psalm *In te domine speravi* ("I have hope in thee O Lord").

St. Nicholas died on 6 December, 343, in Myra and he was buried in his cathedral church. The anniversary of his death later became a day of celebration, St. Nicholas's Day.

Within a century of his death, Nicholas was celebrated as a saint. Today he is venerated in the East as a wonder, or miracle worker, and in the West as patron, friend, and protector of all in trouble or need.

After his death, an impressive church was built over St. Nicholas's crypt and it became one of medieval Europe's great pilgrimage centers.

After the Turks destroyed the city of Myra, they were shown the sepulcher of St. Nicholas. They opened it and found Nicholas' bones swimming in oil. They took his bones away to the city of Bari in 1087.

A liquid formed in St. Nicholas's tomb and became a unique relic, called "Manna," which is renowned for its healing properties. The relics continue to exude this sweet-smelling oil today and its curative powers have encouraged devotion to the saint.

Through the centuries, St. Nicholas has continued to be honored by Orthodox Christians, Catholics, *and* Protestants and he continues to be a role model for the compassionate life.

Widely celebrated throughout Europe, St. Nicholas's feast day, 6 December, kept the stories of his goodness and generosity alive.

Traditionally, in Germany and Poland boys dressed as bishops begged alms for the poor—and sometimes for themselves on St. Nicholas's Eve.

Boy Bishops are often elected in various cathedrals on St. Nicholas's Day because, in 1299, Edward I gave the choristers 40 shillings after hearing the Boy Bishop's service at Heton near Newcastle.

Even the Vikings dedicated their cathedral in Greenland to Nicholas.

On his first voyage, Christopher Columbus named a port in Haiti for St. Nicholas on 6 December, 1492.

The Spaniards named an early settlement in Florida St. Nicholas Ferry. Today it is known as Jacksonville.

By 1500, St. Nicholas was the third most loved religious figure, after Jesus and Mary. There are literally thousands of churches, chapels, and monasteries named after him.

In England St. Nicholas began to be known as the gift-giving Father Christmas in the sixteenth century.

The first Europeans to arrive in the New World brought the tradition of St. Nicholas with them.

The Dutch spelled St. Nicholas "Sint Nikolass," which in the New World became "Sinterklass." This is probably the origin of the saint's most well-known name today— "Santa Claus."

Around the world there is rekindled interest in the original saint as people strive to rediscover the spiritual dimension of Christmas. St. Nicholas had Christ at the center of his life, so who better to put the birth of Jesus back into the center of Christmas?

During his life and in his death, so many miracles have been associated with him that he has become known as "St. Nicholas the Wonderworker."

It is truly remarkable how St. Nicholas, the kind Christian bishop, became the roly-poly, red-suited American symbol of holiday festivity.

He had a broad face and a round little belly,
That shook when he laughed, like a bowl full of jelly,
He was chubby and plump, a right jolly old elf,
And I laughed when I saw him, in spite of myself.

Clement Moore

For little children everywhere
A joyous season still we make;
We bring our precious gifts to them,
Even for the dear child Jesus' sake.

Phoebe Cary

Let the children have their night of fun and laughter, let the gifts of Father Christmas delight their play. Let us grown-ups share to the full in their unstinted pleasures...

Winston Churchill

Santa Claus exists only for those who want to believe in him.

Whether you see him as old St. Nicholas or the jolly old elf in a red suit with white fur lining, Santa Claus still dates back over 1700 years to a bishop who proved his devotion to God and humankind through extraordinary acts of kindness and generosity.

Between 1863 and 1886, the political cartoonist Thomas Nast drew annual pictures of St. Nicholas in *Harper's Weekly*. They were based on the descriptions found in the poem "The Night before Christmas" and may have established the rotund Santa with flowing beard, fur garments, and clay pipe.

According to modern belief, Santa Claus magically travels on a sleigh drawn through the sky by a team of reindeer on Christmas Eve to deliver presents to all the good boys and girls in the world.

In America, Canada, and Britain, Santa Claus slips down the chimney on Christmas Eve to distribute presents under the tree and to fill any stockings that are "hung by the chimney with care."

Santa Claus' reindeer are traditionally called Dasher, Dancer, Prancer, Vixen, Comet, Cupid, Donner, and Blitzen.

The most famous of all the reindeer is Rudolf, who is renowned for his glowing red nose. He will go down in history because he saved Christmas on one foggy Christmas Eve when he used his special, bright nose to guide Santa's sleigh safely.

The legend of flying reindeer is said to relate to a potent hallucinogenic mushroom, called the "fly agaric." It is said that the Lapland herders feed the magic mushrooms to their deer and this gives them the power of flight.

Nothing is said to have demoralized the Confederate army as much as seeing Santa Claus side with the Union soldiers during the American Civil War. It was Abraham Lincoln's idea to have Santa cheer up his troops.

There are as many forms of Santa Claus as there are ways of seeking Christmas.

I stopped believing in Santa Claus when my mother took me to see him in a department store, and he asked for my autograph.

Shirley Temple

In the evening we hung up our stockings…and before dawn we trooped in to open them while sitting on father's and mother's bed; and the bigger presents were arranged, those for each child on its own table, in the drawing-room, the doors to which were thrown open after breakfast. I never knew any one else have what seemed to me such attractive Christmases, and in the next generation I tried to reproduce them exactly for my own children.

Theodore Roosevelt

The bad boys are lining up, hoping to catch a glimpse of Santa's list—of all the naughty girls!

Everyone is free to enter into the spirit of Christmas—as the character Willow in the television program *Buffy The Vampire Slayer* was heard to declare as she handed out presents, "I feel just like Santa Claus, except thinner and younger and female and, well...Jewish."

You know that you're getting old when Santa starts looking younger than you.

Those who always get what they want have little or no need for Santa Claus. Those who love Santa Claus want whatever it is they get from him.

Santa's workshop was built in 1949 on the side of a mountain in a town called North Pole in New York.

A sure way to happiness at Christmas is knowing that you do not require Santa Claus at Christmas but that you secretly long to see him.

The famous poem about Santa Claus known as "The Night Before Christmas" was written by Clement Moore and was intended only for his children and a few guests. Someone sent the poem anonymously to a New York newspaper and it is now known worldwide.

I played Santa Claus many times, and if you don't believe it, check out the divorce settlements awarded my wives.

Groucho Marx

What do you call people who are afraid of Santa Claus?
Claustrophobic.

Why does Santa Claus have three gardens?
So he can hoe, hoe, hoe!

Santa Claus has the right idea:
visit people only once a year.

Victor Borge

Christmas at my house is always at least six or seven times more pleasant than anywhere else. We start drinking early. And while everyone else is seeing only one Santa Claus, we'll be seeing six or seven.

W. C. Fields

Why does Santa always go down the chimney?
Because it soots him!

Who delivers Christmas presents to dogs?
Santa Paws

What kind of motorcycle does Santa ride?
A "Holly" Davidson

What do you call someone who doesn't believe
in Father Christmas?
A rebel without a Claus!

How many chimneys does Santa Claus go down?
Stacks!

I hear that in many places something has happened to Christmas; that it is changing from a time of merriment and carefree gaiety to a holiday which is filled with tedium; that many people dread the day and the obligation to give Christmas presents is a nightmare to weary, bored souls; that the children of enlightened parents no longer believe in Santa Claus; that all in all, the effort to be happy and have pleasure makes many honest hearts grow dark with despair instead of beaming with good will and cheerfulness.

Julia Peterkin

Some see Christmas as a time when children tell Santa Claus what they want and their parents have to pay for it.

Some see Christmas as a cold and lonely place, but so is the North Pole, and Santa lives there!

Yes, Virginia, there is a Santa Claus…Thank God! He lives, and he lives forever. A thousand years from now, Virginia, nay ten times ten thousand years from now, he will continue to make glad the heart of childhood.

Francis Pharcellus Church

There are three ages of man: The first is when he believes in Santa Claus, he reaches the next when he no longer believes in Santa Claus, and the third begins when he has children of his own and he becomes Santa Claus.

In the movie, *Miracle on 34th Street*, a judge ruled that there was a Santa Claus—so it must be true!

If they can put the words "In God we trust" on the back of the American dollar, then every toy car, bicycle, game, and doll should come in a box marked, "In Santa I Believe."

'Twas the night before Christmas, when all through the house
Not a creature was stirring-not even a mouse:
The stockings were hung by the chimney with care,
In hopes that St. Nicholas soon would be there.

Clement C. Moore

If there is no Santa Claus, why are there reindeer tracks on my front lawn and who has been delivering my Christmas presents all these years?

It is easy to get confused about the existence of anything, and when it comes to Santa Claus, you're going to have to trust your heart. However, there is plenty of evidence to suggest that not to believe is as unjustified as any other stance you might take—and it is less than half the fun!

Reflections & Insights

Reflect, as we begin the Advent season, on what is Christmas saying to us that we should be proclaiming?

As Christmas preparations get underway, it is the time to consider what is being celebrated. For some, it will be the holiday of Christmas. For others, it will be the Christ child's birth and the gift of salvation that He brought to earth.

Reflect upon those who are struggling to make ends meet as they face the most expensive time of year.

Consider those, including yourself perhaps, for whom Christmas has never held any "spiritual meaning." Hope that they may come to sense the mystery, awe, and inspiration of it.

Take time to remember all those who are lonely in their homes or confined to hospitals. Pay a call or invite someone round.

Sometimes, in the hurlyburly of it all, one has to steal away to some quiet space to hear the voice of Christmas.

Once the melody of Christmas has entered you, it remains within you forever.

Christmas is to be enjoyed by entertaining friends and loved ones while sharing a few nice surprises and a lot of fond memories.

Until we can feel the spirit of Christmas, there is no Christmas—only display. Look inside yourself.

You won't find Christmas in the air. It is to be found in your own heart and for you to breathe out into the world of men.

Take time to remind yourself of the roots of Christmas and return to contemplate the reason for the season.

Allow yourself to picture in your mind this image: light and joy poured down from heaven together with the joyous message that a child was born.

Silently, the Advent candle grows more potent as it burns ever smaller.

Christmas makes us tender toward the past, brings us hope for the future, and provides us with the courage to face it.

Picture this image: a small group of simple shepherds on a hillside. Imagine their awe as the dark night fills with heavenly light and a band of angels bring them great news.

Christmas teaches us to temper our enjoyments with prudence.

When we enter the Christmas season, we have a tendency just to let things happen rather than try to make them happen.

Christmas in your heart creates frequent attacks of smiling.

Christmas teaches us the lesson of courage: "Man cannot discover new oceans unless he has the courage to lose sight of the shore."

Andre Gide

Christmas teaches us the lesson of faith: "Faith is an oasis in the heart which will never be reached by the caravan of thinking."

Kahlil Gibran

Christmas teaches us the lesson of grace and that no one can disgrace us but ourselves.

Christmas teaches us the lesson of brotherhood and that all men are our brothers.

May the love that we share here now remain between us throughout the coming year.

Amen

Come Lord Jesus, our guest to be, and bless these gifts bestowed by Thee. Amen

We suddenly wake one Christmas morning, and no longer feel the excitement we felt when we were children. We can, and must, rediscover that child inside us. When we do, we will rediscover the magic of Christmas.

Consider the birth,
the song of the angels,
the gladness of the shepherds,
the worship of the wise men.

Put down your burden of care and listen to the songs of angels.

The Christmas heart is a giving heart. Give and forgive.

If peace has a season, then it is Christmas.

And, lo, the angel of the Lord came upon them, and the glory of the Lord shone round about them: and they were sore afraid.

And the angel said unto them, Fear not: for, behold, I bring you good tidings of great joy, which shall be to all people.

For unto you is born this day in the city of David a Saviour, which is Christ the Lord.

Luke 2: 9–11; The Bible

When you throw open your arms to others at Christmas, do so as a welcoming embrace—not one of strangulation.

Christmas is a time for good, a time for kindness and forgiveness. It is a time when all, despite their year-long natures, can unashamedly unlock their hearts, free their charitable spirits, and bask in the sunshine of their own goodwill.

For those of a charitable disposition, there is no more fulfilling a season than Christmas.

I will honor Christmas in my heart, and try to keep it all the year.

Charles Dickens

Of all the days in a year, I can think of no better day for finding forgiveness than Christmas Eve.

A year's kindliness appears vulgar when one attempts to cram it into a single day.

The King of glory sends his Son,
To make his entrance on this earth;
Behold the midnight bright as noon,
And heav'nly hosts declare his birth!
                                        Isaac Watts

The Christmas message goes to those who make time to hear it.

The spirit of Christmas enters our lives when we are able to not see Christmas merely as an event that comes and goes in the course of a day. Then its spirit remains with us all year round.

May the spirit of Christmas inspire all world leaders to ensure the proper welfare of their citizens and renew their determination to defend the great gift of peace.

Christmas is all about the spirit of love. It is a time when all hatred and bitterness toward others should be put aside and our love for our fellow man allowed to prevail.

Turn your thoughts and deeds to the spirit of goodwill, and Christmas will turn its spirit toward you.

For some, Christmas may be about feasting. For many, it is a time for prayer and inner reflection. For all of us, it is a time to remember and be thankful for all that we have loved.

Christmas is not in the outer light show, but in our inner glow.

Christmas—that magic blanket that wraps itself about us— something so intangible—like a fragrance. It weaves a spell of nostalgia and of hope.

Christmas becomes perfect when the things we believe in match the things that we do.

Glory to God in the highest, and on earth peace, good will toward men.

Luke 2:14; The Bible

It's almost Christmas when we discover we have lost interest in judging other people.

What is worse? Christmas or your inability to bear it?

He who seeks Christmas under a tree would do better to look within his own heart. For until he can find it there, he will not find it on this earth.

Christmas belongs to all centuries, to all countries, and to all races.

When all about you are gone into the world of Christmas, do not sit there alone, lingering.

There are three required qualities for making the perfect Christmas: passion, a feeling of responsibility, and a sense of proportion.

Behold, a virgin shall be with child, and shall bring forth a son and they shall call his name Emmanuel, which being interpreted is, God with us.

Matthew 1: 23; The Bible

There is wisdom to entering Christmas with a happy mind, and greatness at this time of year rests with being kind.

With the true Christmas spirit in your heart, there is a smile for everything that may go wrong.

When you become firmly resolved to celebrate Christmas, nothing that chance, destiny,or fate can throw your way can weaken that.

A Christmas without love or friendship as its foundation is as doomed to fail as a skyscraper built on quicksand.

Remind yourself of the true meaning of Christmas by going to see a nativity play at your local school or church.

For Christmas, sow a deed of kindness even though you may never witness the harvest.

Now when Jesus was born in Bethlehem of Judea in the days of Herod the king, behold, there came wise men from the east to Jerusalem, Saying, Where is he that is born King of the Jews? for we have seen his star in the east, and are come to worship him.

Matthew 2:1–2; The Bible

Christmas is about bearing each other's burdens and easing each other's loads.

Christmas reflects all our values, traditions, desires, aspirations, and our affections. It is therefore up to each of us to make it as we would have it be.

Christmas represents the bringing into a sick world of the healing medicine of love.

Few things draw people closer to each other than the warmth of Christmas.

He is less a selfish creature than at any other time; When the Christmas spirit rules him he comes close to the sublime.

Edgar Guest

It's not just about creating the look, nor is it just about the food and drink. It's about the feeling. If you can feel Christmas in your heart, you can spread the feeling all around you.

Awake, glad heart!
Get up and sing!
It is the birth-day of thy King.
Awake! awake!
The Sun doth shake
Light from his locks,
 and all the way
Breathing perfumes,
 doth spice the day.

Henry Vaughan

Christmas is a time when we feel the most homesick. Curiously, this happens even when we are at home!

Let your heart grow tender and become a child again at Christmas.

The more childlike we become at Christmas, the better the spirit we have to face the new year that is to follow.

It seems that the older we get and the closer we come to each Christmas, the deeper the longing we feel for something uncertain—something missed, and yet intangible.

This Christmas, remember this: Your love weighs more than gold.

As you sit with the loved ones of your family, spare a moment to remember those families who are separated and cannot be together at Christmas.

Give yourself over to the spirit of Christmas.

Christmas is a time to be sincere.
"Every man alone is sincere. At the entrance
of a second person, hypocrisy begins."
Ralph Waldo Emerson

Christmas is a time to give proof of humility.
"It was pride that changed angels into devils;
it is humility that makes men as angels."
St. Augustine

Christmas is a time to have faith.
"Faith is the substance of things hoped for,
the evidence of things not seen."
Hebrews 11:1; The Bible

Christmas is a time to love justice.
"Justice consists of doing no one injury, decency
in giving no one offence."

Marcus T. Cicero

Christmas is a time to be merciful.
"Blessed are the merciful; for they shall obtain mercy."

Matthew; The Bible

Christmas is a time to endure persecution.
"Tolerance implies no lack of commitment to
one's own beliefs. Rather it condemns the
oppression or persecution of others."

John F. Kennedy

Christmas is a time to live in truth.
"Whatever satisfies the soul is truth."

Walt Whitman

Christmas is a time to repent of sin. "What is past is past, there is a future left to all men, who have the virtue to repent and the energy to atone."

Edward G. Bulwer-Lytton

Christmas is a time to find spiritual joy and to live without malice, pure of heart."All earthly delights are sweeter in expectation than in enjoyment; but all spiritual pleasures more in fruition than in expectation."

François Fénelon

When the song of angels is stilled,
When the star in the sky is gone,
When the kings and princes are
   home,
When the shepherds are back with
   their flocks,
The work of Christmas begins.
To find the lost, to heal the broken,
   to feed the hungry,
To release the prisoner, to rebuild
   the nations,
To bring peace among others,
To make music in the heart.

Howard Thurman

Christmas is the breeding ground for understanding and sincerity between people.

Jesus often says in the Bible, "Be of good cheer." Perhaps that is why we should endeavour to have and wish others, "A Merry Christmas."

To be happy about Christmas, one must be able to become aware of oneself as part of Christmas without taking fright.

Let the mystery of Christmas become an object of contemplation.

The Christmas we celebrate today has been nurtured over many centuries. It speaks afresh to us each year.

At Christmas, those who talk to God in prayer may be visited by angels. Those who act out their prayers by visiting the sick and lonely may be considered angels themselves.

Look at those things that separate you from Christmas as being your links to it— like two people on opposite sides of a locked gate. It keeps them apart, but they can communicate and reach out to each other through it.

May the Christmas snow remind us of the cleansing power of the Christmas story.

All great mysteries need not inevitably degenerate by turning into beliefs.

May the Christmas bells sounding in glorious proclamation remind us for a few moments at least of the birth of a child in a stable long ago.

May the Christmas carols put us in a frame of mind to put aside our differences and accept the glad tidings proclaimed to mankind.

May the Christmas season remind every one that there is the potential for good, peace, and love in all of us.

What is the true spirit of Christmas? If anything, it is to be plenteous in mercy.

Christmas becomes degraded if we insist upon turning it into an object of affirmation and negation.

We know it's Christmas when our troubled hearts are soothed.

The time draws near the birth of Christ;

The moon is hid; the night is still;

The Christmas bells from hill to hill

Answer each other in the mist.

Alfred, Lord Tennyson

Every year, Christmas arrives more heavily wrapped than the year before. One must tear through many layers in order to get to the real Christmas.

We know we're in the Christmas spirit when we discover that we have an unusual ability to enjoy each moment.

We know it's Christmas when we lose interest in interpreting the actions of others.

If we can promote peace on earth and goodwill to all mankind at Christmas, imagine a world where we promote those feelings every day.

Some people feel ill-equipped or unable to celebrate Christmas. Yet any person alive who believes that love is stronger than hate, more powerful than evil, and capable of surviving beyond death, has Christmas in their heart.

When we are filled with the spirit of Christmas, we are transformed into witnesses of truth, justice, and love.

May the spirit of Christmas inspire us all to overcome the barriers that divide.

If you are feeling alone or lonely and are unable to get into the Christmas spirit, offer your services to your local church or other social charity. Whether it's helping to cook a dinner for pensioners, decorating the church with flowers, or sewing costumes for the children's nativity play, it will put you back in touch with Christmas.

Christmas is for those whose hearts are heavy—may they find joy.

Christmas is for those who walk in darkness—may they find light.

Spend Christmas with a joyous friend.
Shared joy is double joy.

Spend Christmas with a sorrowful
friend. Shared sorrow is half sorrow.

**May the spirit of Christmas inspire everyone
to become charitable, understanding, and
pardoning toward those they believe to have
done them wrong.**

May the spirit of Christmas inspire everyone to accept
all peoples as their brothers and sisters. One people,
on one planet, sowing peace forever.

But while he thought on these things, behold, the angel of the Lord appeared unto him in a dream, saying, "Joseph, thou son of David, fear not to take unto thee Mary thy wife: for that which is conceived in her is of the Holy Ghost. And she shall bring forth a son, and thou shalt call his name JESUS: for he shall save his people from their sins."

Matthew 1: 20–21; The Bible

We know it's almost Christmas when we discover that we have a tendency to think and act spontaneously and are not constrained by fears based upon past experiences.

Christmas is a time for healing emotional pain. First identify your feelings and then allow yourself to feel them.

At Christmas, if we define ourselves in terms of our past suffering, we will inevitably remain in pain.

Remove your attention from painful memories that hold you in emotional pain—then you will be free of that pain.

If as many people kept Christ's commandments as celebrate his birthday, what a peaceful world this would be!

With the Christmas spirit come overwhelming episodes of appreciation.

Christmas provides us with contented feelings of connectedness with others and nature.

Christmas creates in us a susceptibility to the love extended by others and the uncontrollable urge to extend it ourselves.

The spirit is at home at Christmas and rarely entirely satisfied elsewhere.

Everyone has as much right as he has might to celebrate Christmas.

It is perfectly possible to go through life not knowing if God exists or why He should exist. Believers and non-believers share this world and live in it in a state of history—the birth of Christ is a pivotal point in world history.

Those who find Christmas in their heart also find gratitude for every day of life—for each encounter of love and every moment of peace.

Christmas is a time of miracles. There are always miracles where there is love.

Christmas is a holy and magical time. Find a moment for a prayer for peace. If you cannot pray, make a wish for peace instead.

Take time out from Christmas. Even a few well-chosen minutes away from the festivities will help you to appreciate it even more.

Myths,
Legends, &
Superstitions

Superstition has it that children born on Christmas Day will have a special fortune.

It is said that wearing new shoes on Christmas Day will bring bad luck.

The Christmas wreath, made in a circle from holly and other evergreens, is a neverending symbol of eternal hope.

There is a legend that at midnight on Christmas Eve, all cattle rise in their stalls or kneel to adore the newborn King.

In the North of England, people used to believe that bees assembled on Christmas Eve to hum a Christmas hymn.

There is a superstition that says if you eat plum pudding at Christmas, you'll avoid losing a friend before next Christmas.

Mexican legends know the poinsettia as "Flower of the Holy Night." A peasant girl who wanted to go to Midnight Mass couldn't afford a gift for Jesus so an angel appeared and told her to take some weeds with her. When she arrived, the top leaves turned scarlet red.

There is an old wives' tale that says bread baked on Christmas Eve will never go moldy.

The Christmas wreath should be hung on the first day of Advent and stay in place at least through Twelfth Night.

Twelfth Night, 6 January, has been celebrated since the Middle Ages as one of the most important days in the Christian calendar, the Feast of the Epiphany. It marks the arrival in Bethlehem of the Wise Men, or Magi, who brought the infant Jesus gifts.

Over time, the Three Wise Men have became known as the Three Kings. Caspar brought the gift of frankincense for divinity, Melchior brought the gift of gold for kingship, and Balthazar gave myrrh for humanity.

A child that's born on a Christmas Day, is fair and wise, good and gay.

Anonymous

There was a tradition for young women to cut a branch from a cherry or pear tree on December 4, St. Barbara's Day, and place it in lukewarm water next to the fire. If the branch bloomed on Christmas Eve, she would soon marry.

The tradition of decorating with evergreens, berries, and winter flowers goes back to pagan times. These plants were believed to hold mystical powers because they retained signs of life in midwinter.

In England people began to bring Christmas trees into their homes after Prince Albert brought a decorated Christmas tree back from Germany for Queen Victoria and their children.

Candles and Christmas tree lights symbolize the Light coming into the world.

In England, even bees were once wished "A Merry Christmas" by their keepers decorating their hives with a sprig of holly.

Enemy soldiers who met under the mistletoe plant during Roman times would lay down their weapons, cease fighting, and embrace one another.

Stars that shine bright on Christmas Eve will make hens lay plenty of eggs.

Proverb

French peasants believed that babies who come into the world on Christmas Day are born with the gift of prophecy.

The Church used holly as a substitute for mistletoe. It became a symbol of Christ—the sharp leaves represent his crown of thorns, and the red berries symbolize his blood.

One legend tells how the newborn baby Jesus was shivering from the cold so a little bird flew down to fan the nearby fire with its wings to warm him. The fire scorched the bird, and this is how the robin came to have its red breast.

Some people consider mistletoe to be a magical plant that keeps evil spirits at bay, but others regard it as a good excuse to steal a kiss!

A silver coin (traditionally a farthing) is sometimes hidden in the plum pudding because it is said to bring wealth, health, and happiness to the person who finds it.

You must eat twelve mince pies over the Christmas period to ensure prosperity for each of the ensuing twelve months.

The first person to open the front door on Christmas morning will prosper in the coming year.

The last Sunday before Advent is known to some as "Stir Up Sunday" and it's the day to make Christmas wishes when you stir the Christmas pudding.

On "Stir Up Sunday" everyone must take a turn stirring the Christmas pudding to make the household prosper. You should stir at least three times, seeing the bottom of the pot each time, and making a wish that's kept secret until it comes true.

If you entwine holly and ivy in your decorations at Christmas it is supposed to ensure peace between husband and wife in the year ahead.

Superstition drove people to bring in their plow and keep it under the dining table for the duration of the Christmas season.

"As goes Christmas Eve, so goes the year" is a saying in many countries. It suggests that if everyone is polite, generous, and forgiving on December 24, we can look forward to a good year.

In Ireland it is believed that the gates of heaven open at midnight on Christmas Eve and that those who die during this period go straight to heaven, by passing purgatory.

If you take a candle to church at Christmas, you should not bring it home. Blow it out and leave it with the vicar for good luck.

On New Year's Day it is considered bad luck if the first visitor at your house has red hair. Good luck comes if a stranger with black hair knocks at the door.

Some farmers used to cut their animals to make them bleed on the day after Christmas. They believed that bloodletting would improve their livestock's health and stamina in the coming year.

There is a legend that when Mary washed out baby Jesus's swaddling cloths, she hung them to dry on a small, flowerless bush. The rosemary bush then grew its first tiny, blue flowers; it does so to this day in memory of the occasion.

Out of the mighty Yule log came
The crooning of the lithe wood-flame,—
A single bar of music fraught
With cheerful yet half pensive thought,—
A thought elusive: out of reach,
Yet trembling on the verge of speech.

William Hamilton Hayne

**The Yule log was traditionally burned throughout Europe
to keep the demons away.**

It is seen as bad luck to keep your Christmas trimmings up after Twelfth Night and, therefore, it is best to take them all down before the end of 5 January.

Lending anything, even a thimble or a candle, on New Year's Day is considered unlucky.

Christmas Eve is a time of family gathering and reconciliation throughout the world. It's also a night of magic and, in some countries, people are said to suddenly gain the power to tell the future.

In England Christmas Eve used to be a popular time for "Mummers" to perform plays. At a strategic moment, Father Christmas would burst in: "In comes I, Olde Father Christmas Welcome be or welcome not I hope that Father Christmas Will never be forgot…"

There is a legend that relates that all animals are given the power to speak on Christmas Eve—but it is considered to be bad luck to test the superstition.

The glow worm is said to have come into being when an ordinary little worm gave Jesus a small green leaf. The baby, liking the gift, touched the worm and it began to glow.

It is said that we drape webs of tinsel around the Christmas tree to remember a helpful spider that wove a web across the entrance to a cave to hide the Holy Family from King Herod's soldiers.

Superstition promises that you'll be assured of a bumper crop if you bury the ashes from your Christmas Yule log with your plant seeds in the spring.

At Christmas, if any young maid wants to learn her future husband's trade, she should reach into a river and grab the first thing she touches. If it's an old shoe, he'll be a cobbler; a piece of wood, a carpenter; metal, a blacksmith; and so on.

In the days before salmonella scares, it was believed that if you ate a raw egg before anything else on Christmas morning, you would magically be able to carry heavy weights.

A sunny Christmas Eve brings fair weather all year round.

Proverb

In some rural areas of Ireland, people still observe the custom of cleaning their houses to purify everything in honor of the birth of Christ—this is said to have evolved from an ancient Mesopotamian tradition.

You can also discover who you will marry by washing your face, but not drying it, before going to bed on Christmas Eve. Hang a towel at the end of the bed—the person who hands you the towel in your dreams will be your true intended!

**Never fear snow at Christmas—
it means Easter will be green.**

The Christmas rose flowers at Christmas as a reminder
of the purity of the Virgin Mary. Spanish legend tells of
a young shepherdess who cried because she was too
poor to take a gift to the baby Jesus. Her tears fell to
the ground and the Christmas rose grew.

**Good luck will come to the
home where a fire has been
kept burning throughout
the Christmas season.**

One should always place shoes side by side on Christmas Eve to ensure that the family will not quarrel during the festive season.

It is said that a clear star-filled sky on Christmas Eve will bring good crops in the summer.

If the Christmas tree sinks in water, the egg rolls on ice.

Proverb

A blowing wind on Christmas Day is said to bring good luck.

In some parts of England, it is said that a girl can find out if she's going to marry in the coming year by banging on the henhouse door on Christmas Eve. If a rooster crows, the answer is yes.

You will have as many happy months in the coming year as the number of houses in which you eat mince pies during Christmas time.

In pagan times, mistletoe played an important role in both Celtic Druidism and the Asgardian myths of Scandinavia. The Druids knew it as "All Heal" and believed it brought good luck and fertility and also offered protection against witchcraft.

The Twelve Days of Christmas traditionally begin on the day after Christmas—known as Boxing Day—and end on Twelfth Night.

In Celtic countries New Year's Eve—Scottish Hogmanay—has always taken priority over Christmas as a time for warding off evil spirits and encouraging the sun to return.

The tradition of carolling dates back to ancient Greece. The word choraulien means "to dance to a flute," but by the Middle Ages it had changed to mean "to sing and dance together."

7 and 12 January are traditionally St. Distaff's days, in honor of the blessed spinning tool used by women who return to work after the Christmas festivities on one of these days.

Good King Wenceslas, he of the carol, was a mysterious Bohemian nobleman of the tenth century who was murdered by his mother and brother at the age of 26.

The term "Christmas box" goes back to the days when churches used to collect money in boxes to give to the poor. This took place on the day after Christmas Day, which is why 26 December is now known as Boxing Day.

Carol singers traditionally arrived with brooms on their shoulders to sweep good luck into the houses they were visiting.

Mistletoe was originally hung above doors to ward off evil and to give fairies shelter from the frost.

The doors of a house should be opened wide at midnight on Christmas Eve to let out any trapped evil spirits.

Many homes in Ireland still display a lit candle in a window on Christmas Eve. The candle welcomes strangers, and not showing a light means that you, like the innkeepers in Bethlehem, have no room for them.

Twelfth Night celebrations were particularly popular during the eighteenth and nineteenth centuries. "Twelfth cake," the forerunner of today's Christmas cake, was central to the feasting and one dried bean and one dried pea were hidden in it. The man and woman who discovered these were elected King and Queen for the night.

The tradition of placing charms in the plum pudding probably evolved from putting dried beans and peas into the Twelfth cake.

In the Scottish Highlands, holly is hung in the house to ward off mischievous fairies. It was also believed to be lucky for men, while ivy was lucky for women.

If prickly holly is brought into the home first, it will be a male-dominated year. If smooth holly or ivy are brought in first, the female will rule the roost.

Before Christianity reached them, the pagans recognized "Saturnalia" from December 17 to 24. The feasting and merrymaking ended on December 25, when they celebrated the rebirth of the sun god.

If you listened to the animals on Christmas Eve, their conversation might be this: Owl asks "Whooo?" was born and Raven answers "Christ." Goat asks "Where?" and Lamb faces the stable and answers "There!"

In Scotland trinkets were once baked inside the Yule breads to tell people's fortunes.

A "Jesse tree" is traditionally decorated with ornaments associated with Old Testament events, and in some churches a Jesse tree is used to collect clothing for the poor.

Young women seeking to know their marital future traditionally based their predictions on the sky's aura between Christmas Eve and Twelfth Night.

Animals weren't mentioned in the Christmas story until a carol appeared describing how a donkey carried Mary to Bethlehem and how the other animals cared for her and the baby in the stable.

Because it was considered a symbol of good luck, farmers used to hang holly in their cowsheds on Christmas Eve to ensure a good supply of milk during the coming year.

In England the definition of a white Christmas is when one snowflake falls on the roof of the London Weather Center. So far, there have been only seven or eight on record!

St. Francis of Assisi introduced Christmas carols into formal church services.

The figures of the Three Kings are not supposed to be added to the Christmas crib until Twelfth Night, also known as "Three Kings' Day."

A rosemary bush, a date palm, and a sugar cane argued about which of them was most important to the Holy Family. The palm said it offered shade and fruits, the sugar cane said it offered sweetness and refreshing drinks, and the rosemary bush said nothing. Then Mary came out to hang out some washing; she couldn't reach the top of the palm and the washing slid off the sugar cane, so she placed the clothes on the bush. "Perfect," she said, and since then the rosemary has borne flowers the color of her gown.

In Victorian England postmen were known as "robins," possibly because their uniforms were red. Christmas cards of the time often showed a robin delivering mail.

A shine on the birth of our Savior will be seen throughout January.

Proverb

The Glastonbury Thorn legend tells that a wooden staff that Joseph of Arimathea pushed into the ground while spreading Jesus's message in Britain took root and blossomed. It has flowered every Christmas and spring since, and a cutting of the original thorn grows at Glastonbury Abbey today.

The judge the festival of Christmas near,
Christmas, the joyous season of the year.
Now with bright holly all your temples strow,
With laurel green, and sacred mistletoe.

John Gay

Christmas cards were first sent during the Victorian era when the "penny post" public postal deliveries began. Christmas cards cost only half a penny to send.

When a disgruntled Joseph was asked by his pregnant wife Mary to pick her a cherry, he told her to get the father of her child to pick her cherries for her. With that, God made the cherry tree bow down so that she could help herself, and Joseph's mind was finally at peace.

The Twelve Days of Christmas was the main festival of Elizabethan England, a period when people were encouraged to welcome the poor by providing food, shelter, and good cheer during the cold, bleak winter.

December 31 is New Year's Eve or Old Year's Night. Today it is still a time for divination, fortune telling, and making resolutions.

The sky's aura between Christmas Eve and Twelfth Night was sometimes read by farmers and elderly people as an indication of the weather for the year ahead.

There is a belief that one should try to repay all debts before the New Year because ending a year in debt means a whole new year of debt.

One Twelfth Night tradition is wassailing, meaning "be whole." Hot ale or cider laced with nutmeg, roasted apples, and sugar is drunk from a large wassail bowl, then people sing to the trees or fire shotguns into their branches to ensure a healthy crop!

10 January or the Monday following Twelfth Night is traditionally the day to return to work after the Christmas festivities, and is known as "Plow Monday." A plow used to be blessed in church then dragged through the streets, and a gift of money was given to servants by their employers.

Wren hunts were traditionally popular on 26 December or Boxing Day. The king of the birds, the wren, was hunted and caged in a small "wren house" and then paraded through the town.

In Wales the "Mari Lwyd" tradition is based on a legend of a horse that was turned out of the stable to make way for Mary, Joseph, and Jesus. A decorated horse's skull is paraded around the village and verses are sung to the inhabitants of each home in question-and-answer format.

It is said that a holly tree stood outside the Bethlehem stable in which Jesus was born. Birds had eaten all the berries off it, but the tree budded, flowered, and bore berries at his birth.

Cutting a branch on 4 December, St. Barbara's Day, to see if it blooms by Christmas Eve is a way to test one's good luck.

An Advent wreath has four candles, one of which is a different color from the others to mark the third Sunday. A candle is lit on each of the four Sundays in Advent before Christmas.

Early Christian leaders incorporated the pagans' winter festival into the Christian calendar, slowly changing its meaning, which is why Christ's birth is now celebrated on 25 December.

Today a silver coin, a thimble, and a ring are often stirred into the Christmas pudding—the coin brings luck to the person who finds it, the thimble prosperity, and the ring a wedding or marital bliss.

Sweep the floor from the door toward the hearth on New Year's Day. If dust is swept toward the door, it's thought that luck is swept outside for the year.

It wasn't until about 200 years after Christ's death that the Christians even thought about celebrating his birth.

There is hidden depth to the carol "The Twelve Days of Christmas." It was written at a time when Catholics risked their lives if they were caught practicing their faith, so they used metaphors to mask the true religious meaning.

On the first day of Christmas
My true love sent to me
A partridge in a pear tree.
This symbolizes Jesus Christ, a partridge
protecting its nestlings.

On the second day of Christmas
My true love sent to me
Two turtle doves.
These symbolize the Old and the New
Testaments.

On the third day of Christmas
My true love sent to me
Three French hens.
These symbolize the Christian virtues
of faith, hope, and charity.

On the fourth day of Christmas
My true love sent to me
Four calling birds.

These symbolize the four Gospels:
Matthew, Mark, Luke, and John.

On the fifth day of Christmas
My true love sent to me
Five gold rings.

These recall the Torah or Law, the first
five books of the Old Testament.

On the sixth day of Christmas
My true love sent to me
Six geese a-laying.
**These symbolize the six days
of creation.**

On the seventh day of Christmas
My true love sent to me
Seven swans a-swimming.
**These symbolize the seven gifts of
the Holy Spirit: prophecy, serving,
teaching, exhortation, contribution,
leadership, and mercy.**

On the eighth day of Christmas
My true love sent to me
Eight maids a-milking.
These symbolize the eight Beatitudes as
given by Jesus in the Gospel of Matthew.

On the ninth day of Christmas
My true love sent to me
Nine ladies dancing.
These symbolize the nine fruits of the
Holy Spirit: love, joy, peace, patience,
kindness, goodness, faithfulness,
gentleness, and self-control.

On the tenth day of Christmas

My true love sent to me

Ten lords a-leaping.

These symbolize the Ten Commandments.

On the eleventh day of Christmas

My true love sent to me

Eleven pipers piping.

These symbolize the eleven
faithful Apostles.

On the twelfth day of Christmas
My true love sent to me
Twelve drummers drumming.

**These symbolize the twelve points
of belief in the Apostles' Creed.**

Food &
Feasting

When it comes to Christmas dinners, dream big and dare to fail.

The secret to a stress-free Christmas meal is detailed planning and preparation. Try to keep a calm head while you're cooking and remember that a turkey takes a very long time to cook.

Plan your gathering knowing how you want it to go. If you want to have some fun entertainment, check out which of your friends can play the piano for carol singing, who might be fun at charades, and which ones have amusing anecdotes for after dinner.

Get a few of your friends involved in the work in the kitchen. This will allow you to socialize and enjoy the preparations so much more—somehow, gravy made in good company always tastes much better.

Add these little touches: handwritten place cards, seasonal napkins, runners over the chair backs, and candles strategically placed in alcoves or near reflective objects and shiny surfaces.

Always lay your dinner table on Christmas Eve—you'll have enough to worry about in the kitchen on the day without having to hunt for matching napkins or the correct assortment of cutlery.

Arranging the dinner table is a great way to get the kids involved in the preparations. They can choose the color scheme, organize the place settings, or make fun seasonal place cards shaped like Christmas trees, reindeer, angels, or Santa Claus.

Treat the taste buds and the stomachs of your nearest and dearest with a wonderful traditional spread—complete with all the trimmings.

Make a small and simple Yule log centerpiece: Drill a hole the diameter of the candle you'll use into a small log and set a candle into it. Sprinkle it with powdered sugar, place a couple of sprigs of holly on it, and it will make the table look Christmassy.

Remember that the secret of a beautiful display lies in the details, so go all out when preparing the Christmas table. Make your glasses and cutlery gleam.

Fill old crystal wine glasses with some glass beads, a couple of holly leaves, and some holly berries. Stand a candle in each, and you've got instant seasonal atmosphere.

Fill the house with a delightful Christmas aroma by simmering a pot of water in which you have placed some cinnamon sticks and citrus fruit.

**Bear in mind that the most simple meal can look
á la carte when it is well presented and served on
attractive platters.**

The coach was crowded, both inside

and out, with passengers, who, by their

talk, seemed principally bound to the

mansions of relations or friends, to eat

Christmas dinner…

Washington Irving

**Remember that what matters isn't what's on the
table but who is in the chairs.**

Creating seasonal centerpieces for a table can be fun for older children. Try combining small evergreen branches, peeling birch twigs, and some bare hardwood twigs you've sprayed white. Add a sprinkling of gold glitter and a few sprigs of red berries.

Praise be to the mother who, as she sees her child drop the turkey to the floor under the horrified gaze of everyone at the table, calmly collects the bird from the floor and says confidently and reassuringly to her offspring, "Never mind darling, let's go into the kitchen and get the other one."

Create a Christmas dry snack masterpiece. Drizzle some tasty nut oil over a selection of freshly shelled nuts, and sprinkle some garam masala over them. Toss until the nuts are evenly coated. Spread them out on a cookie sheet and roast for 15 minutes. The smell and the taste will drive everybody nuts!

A lovely extra touch is to prepare decorative menu cards and place them on the table before dinner. Your guests will have a sneak preview of the meal to tantalize their taste buds.

Another delightful touch is to fill a large, sparkling glass bowl with water. Then add a few drops of food coloring to the water, and carefully float some lit candles on the surface.

If you refuse a mince pie at Christmas dinner, you will have bad luck for the coming day.

English saying

As you sit down to dine on Christmas Day, spare a thought for those dealing with emergencies and those who provide essential services.

We should remind ourselves of what we are celebrating as we come together for dinner by saying a short blessing or prayer of thanks.

On this joyful day, may the light of Christmas illuminate our hearts and shine in our words and deeds. May the hope, the peace, the joy, and the love of Christmas fill our lives and become part of all we say and do. Bless us and the feast provided for us and let us be thankful for the gift of Christmas.

Christmas is coming, the geese are getting fat
Please to put a penny in the old man's hat;
If you haven't got a penny, a ha'penny will do,
If you haven't got a ha'penny, then God bless you!

Traditional verse

How do you want to spend your Christmas? All day and night in the kitchen unable to socialize? Simplify wherever possible and ask other people to help with easy tasks.

Remember one key fact at all times: The simple things in life bring the greatest joy. Your nearest and dearest would much prefer a heartfelt embrace and the words "I love you" to your spending all your energy creating an elaborate ice sculpture!

Never make your Christmas preparations an obvious bid for popularity. You entertain because you want to be among friends. People come because they want to share Christmas with you. Don't turn your special gathering into a dreadful, over-the-top dinner party.

Concentrate—if you're preparing a sumptuous feast, don't focus your attention on a monstrously large floral arrangement and then discover, too late, that you were supposed to take the giblets out of the bird!

If you place your candles in the freezer for a couple of hours before you serve dinner, they won't drip on your tablecloth so much.

The danger is that people will take excesses as ostentation rather than affection!

And Jesus said unto them, I am the bread of life: he that cometh to me shall never hunger; and he that believeth on me shall never thirst.

John 6:35; The Bible

Christmas has everybody's vote, except perhaps the turkeys'.

Experiment with homemade ice creams in a variety of flavors. As Voltaire said, ice cream "...is exquisite. What a pity it isn't illegal."

Take care to prepare enough for everybody to have seconds because as François Rabelais said, "The appetite grows by eating."

Fed up with turkey? Try a traditional English roast beef, but take heed of William Shakespeare: "I am a great eater of beef, and I believe that does harm to my wit."

A few party tidbits and a bit of lingering over a drink before dinner puts an edge on everyone's appetite. As Cervantes commented, "Hunger is the best sauce in the world."

Feasting brings on fatigue. Be prepared to stimulate the table back to life by serving the very best coffee available at the end of your Christmas meal.

If you plan to serve a turkey, give yourself time to research the very best method of preparing it. As David Garrick observed, "Heaven sends us good meat, but the Devil sends cooks."

At Christmas, enjoy the excess but avoid gluttony.

Always ensure that your guests have an elegant sufficiency. As Sydney Smith wrote, "Serenely full, the epicure would say, Fate cannot harm me, I have dined to-day."

The key to success for having the perfect Christmas meal is simply meticulous planning.

Christmas is the time for heady overindulgence. Many a strange and wonderful Christmas dream is born from smoked salmon struggling upstream against a current of claret and mincemeat.

Do not feel compelled to stretch yourself beyond your culinary capabilities because to most people a simple, home-cooked meal is always the best. Even Prince Philip once commented, "I never see any home cooking. All I get is fancy stuff."

Remember that presentation is everything. Winston Churchill famously said, "Take away that pudding—it has no theme."

Serve seasonal coffee, never instant. Use a French press and allow a tablespoon of freshly ground hazelnut-flavored coffee per cup.

When decorating the table, remember that your Yuletide centerpiece is likely to take up a lot of space.

My grandmother used to make gravy with a cigarette perched between her lips. The ash would grow in size until inevitably it fell unnoticed into the pan. Unaware, she'd continue to stir, and we children watched in amusement at Christmas dinner when the grown-ups savored the delicate, exotic flavor of her brew.

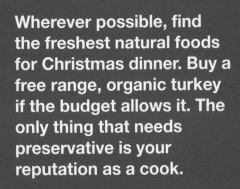

Jonathan Swift recommended that when cooking, "If a lump of soot falls into the soup and you cannot conveniently get it out, stir it well in and it will give the soup a French taste."

Wherever possible, find the freshest natural foods for Christmas dinner. Buy a free range, organic turkey if the budget allows it. The only thing that needs preservative is your reputation as a cook.

Give a frozen turkey plenty of time to defrost—don't expect to thaw it and cook it on the same day!

Out to the table it comes, the traditional Christmas turkey in all its glory—like a plump missionary being served to a tribe of ravening cannibals.

I refuse to spend my life worrying about what I eat. There's no pleasure worth forgoing just for an extra three years in the geriatric ward.

John Mortimer

I think this idea of Henry Miller is a most unfair image of the nation that gave the world the turkey! "Americans will eat garbage provided you sprinkle it liberally with ketchup."

What better beverage for a day of writing Christmas cards than a big jug of hot chocolate? As Baron Justus von Liebig suggested, "...it is the best friend of those engaged in literary pursuits."

The excesses of Christmas have a tendency to overwhelm. Be careful not to dig your own grave with your teeth!

Candles and flowers for the table should not be scented. If they are, they're likely to overpower the aromas and flavors of the food.

Create lovely place cards for the table by writing them by hand or using a special font on the computer.

For a striking seasonal centerpiece, use wooden kebab skewers and toothpicks to construct a pyramid of tangerines or clementines. Intersperse natural leaves from a citrus tree if you have them, or fresh holly or bay leaves.

For a simple yet elegant centerpiece that will make good use of your spare decorations, fill an attractive glass bowl with bright Christmas balls in seasonal colors—red, gold, and green are best.

Always remember to keep your centerpieces and candles low, so that people can talk across the table without peering through a forest of greenery!

To make surprise gift nuts, split some large, well-shaped walnuts. Remove the nut meats and put small trinkets inside the shells. Glue a piece of narrow ribbon to one end of a shell, glue the two halves of the shells together, and mix them with other walnuts in a bowl. Allow one gift nut for each guest.

Put your leftovers to work and make a Christmas Wenceslas pizza.
How did Good King Wenceslas like his pizzas?
Deep pan, crisp and even!

In Austria your Christmas Eve dinner might consist of braised carp in a ginger and beer sauce with crepes of sweet cheese baked in a custard topped with apricot coulis.

The atmosphere in a Belgian house on Christmas Eve will be filled with spiced cookies flavored with ginger, cinnamon, and cloves mingled with the smell of frying potato rissoles and the heavenly aroma of beeswax candles.

Oddly enough, there are no plums in a traditional English plum pudding. It's named for the process of "plumming," or plumping up, the raisins and currants in it by soaking them in warm brandy.

Christmas pudding is at its very best served hot and flamed with brandy, topped off with a decorative sprig of holly and accompanied by "harde sauce," otherwise known as brandy butter.

The plum-pudding was of the same handsome roundness as ever, and came in with the symbolic blue flames around it, as if it had been heroically snatched from the nether fires, into which it had been thrown by dyspeptic Puritans.

George Eliot

In some regions of France, after a wonderful roast goose you might be surprised by the arrival of a "*Bûche de Nöel*," a marvellous cake filled with chestnut cream and coated in marzipan, which was inspired by the ritual of burning a Yule log throughout Christmas Eve.

"Fröhliche Weihnachten from Germany, where you can expect to come home from church on Christmas Eve to strong German coffee and *"Stollen"* cake with its fruit, dry texture, and aromatic flavor.

Stollen cakes have been baked since the fourteenth century to resemble the baby Jesus wrapped in swaddling cloths.

"Zalig Kerstfeest" from Holland, where during Christmas addictive deep-fried, bite-sized flour and raisin pastries called "oliebollen" are served piping hot, sprinkled with powdered sugar.

"Nodlaig Nait Cugat" from Ireland, where Christmas starts with a massive "fry-up"—a breakfast of fried eggs and bacon, mushrooms, and black pudding—that leaves very little room for the roasted ham, turkey, or spiced beef that arrives later in the day, to be washed down, no doubt, with a glass of Guinness.

***"Buon Natale"* from Italy, where the build-up to Christmas is fueled by a diet of pork sausage and lentils and, of course, the rich and exotic panettone cake!**

"Boas Festas" from Portugal, where the national feast is a tasty and distinctive dish known as *"bacalhau"* that's based on dried codfish. It's followed by a dessert of egg- and wine-soaked bread dredged in sugar and fried until it forms a candied crust.

The Scandinavians serve a feast of roasted goose, ham, pickled herring, and rice pudding for Christmas Day.

"Felices Navidades" from Spain, where the ancient nougat-like sweet **"turrón,"** made of honey and almonds, is served. On the big day itself, a big sea bass is roasted with onions and lemons, drizzled with olive oil, and dredged in breadcrumbs.

In Sweden and Denmark a Christmas bread, shaped like a boar, is made from the last corn harvested. This "Yule Boar" stands on the table throughout the season and when spring planting time comes, the farmer mixes part of it with the seed-corn and gives the rest to his workhorse and himself to eat—this assures a good harvest in the fall.

In Poland Christmas dinner might consist of whiskey toast, *pierogi*, beef roll-ups, and Christmas *borscht*, with Christmas bread cake or Christmas pudding.

A glass of mulled apple cider with orange and ginger warms a chilled heart. In a stainless steel pot, combine 8 cups of natural apple cider, a cinnamon stick, a dozen whole cloves, a sliced and peeled orange, and a few slices of fresh ginger. Simmer for 30 minutes and serve warm.

No turkey dinner would be complete without a side dish of chilled cranberry sauce. Wash fresh cranberries, put them in a large pot with 1 cup of granulated sugar and 1 cup of apricot brandy. Simmer for 40 minutes on a medium/low heat. Take off the heat and chill the sauce for at least 2 hours before serving. A squeeze of lemon juice adds pizzazz to the final product.

If you are roasting potatoes, a good tip is to parboil them for 7 or 8 minutes, then shake them and sprinkle with salt. Let them cool, then pop them into the oven 1 hour before serving, turning once, and they'll be beautifully crisp.

If you don't have time to cook your own Christmas pudding, buy a pre-made one and add a personal touch: Put a coin or lucky trinket that you've washed carefully into the pudding, while making a wish. Then garnish the pudding with a decorative sprig of holly. Pour over some warmed brandy, strike a match, and "Voilà!"

A good Christmas whiskey punch is easy to make. Mix ¼ cup of brown sugar and 2 cups of whiskey. Heat just enough to dissolve the sugar, and pour into mugs. Put a slice of lemon and 3 or 4 whole cloves in each mug and add hot water to taste.

Give sprouts a chance this Christmas. Remove the outer leaves and score the ends. Wash them well, then place them in boiling salted water to simmer for about 5 minutes. Drain them, refreshing them in cold water, then, just before serving, pop them back into boiling water just long enough to reheat. Drain again, toss in butter, grind over some pepper, and serve. They will complement the turkey perfectly with a fresh nutty taste.

Christmas pudding may have originated from a fourteenth-century "porridge" called "frumenty." Similar to a soup, it was made by boiling beef and mutton with raisins, currants, prunes, wines, and spices, and was a fasting dish eaten in preparation for Christmas festivities.

A delicious Christmas tipple is mulled cider with Calvados. In a stainless steel pot, combine apple cider, brown sugar to taste, a little allspice, and freshly ground nutmeg, 4 or 5 whole cloves, a couple of cinnamon sticks, and a peeled and sliced apple. Simmer this mixture for 15 minutes and add Calvados to taste. When it's hot, pour it through a sieve into mugs, and enjoy!

"Harde sauce" is the traditional accompaniment for a plum pudding. It's made by beating butter, sugar, and brandy—although it could be rum or whiskey—together until smooth and creamy. Chill in the refrigerator until it's "harde." Today, it's called "brandy butter," but its roots stretch back to medieval times.

Roaring fires, rich food, exotic cocktails, an array of wines, strenuous games, late nights, yet more food, candies, liqueurs, cigars.... Be prepared for some undesirable after effects—with luck, the worst will be only a bout of indigestion.

Ask yourself whether the time you spend preparing some foods outweighs using a pre-made version of the same dish!

Roast turkey with all the trimmings is the most important course at Christmas, so keep the others simple. If you are making a starter, choose something easy that you can prepare in advance, which will leave you free to concentrate on the main course.

The simplest starter is a tasty soup. It can be made well in advance and just needs heating up for a few minutes when you are ready to eat.

Plan your time so that the turkey is ready half an hour before you dine. This gives the meat time to relax and you time to make a wonderful gravy.

Place small dishes filled with nuts, fruit, candy, and cookies around the house so that your guests have something to nibble on while they are waiting for the main event.

Some novice cooks find that a practice run a few weeks before helps things to run smoothly on the big day.

Always plan your meal in fine detail and figure out exactly how long everything will take to cook before you start—the simplest matters of pre-planning and thought can prevent all manner of disasters.

Don't forget to check that you have enough platters, serving dishes, and serving spoons for everything you are cooking before you start.

A jug of eggnog is as seasonal as it gets! This rich, creamy drink traditionally made with rum and eggs— and not forgetting the essential fresh nutmeg grated on top—is a perfect Christmas Eve treat.

Any drink that contains rum can be called a "nog," after "grog." The first eggnog made in America was allegedly consumed in Captain John Smith's 1607 Jamestown settlement.

Gingerbread and Christmas go hand in hand. The tradition of making gingerbread houses began in Germany and has since traveled with European settlers all over the world. Recipes for simple gingerbread houses are widely available, so why not have a go at making your own this year?

German *"Lebkuchen,"* or gingerbread, has been around since the 1390s and in the sixteenth century, master bakers in Nuremberg began to press their spiced gingerbread into intricately carved moulds with Christmas motifs.

Wishing to continue their Christmas traditions, German settlers in North America reinvented their recipes using whatever ingredients they could find, such as maple syrup in New England or molasses further south.

Don't go to the grocery store without a list, or shop when you're hungry. Be a clever shopper, too—buy non-perishables when they're on sale so that you can have them to hand later.

There were pears and apples clustered high in blooming pyramids; there were bunches of grapes, made, in the shopkeepers' benevolence, to dangle from conspicuous hooks that people's mouths might water gratis as they passed; there were piles of filberts, mossy and brown, recalling, in their fragrance, ancient walks among the woods, and pleasant shufflings ankle deep through withered leaves; there were Norfolk Biffins, squab and swarthy, setting off the yellow of the oranges and lemons, and, in the great compactness of their juicy persons, urgently entreating and beseeching to be carried home in paper bags and eaten after dinner.

Charles Dickens

In France, after Midnight Mass on Christmas Eve, many people still gather for a feast called *"le réveillon."* It consists of oysters, snails, seafood, smoked salmon, and caviar followed by roasted goose, fine wine, and the traditional Yule Log cake known as *"La Bûche de Noël."*

Each year, famous diarist Samuel Pepys noted with mixed pleasure what he ate at Christmas. In 1662, with his wife seriously ill, he muddled through on a diet of "a mess of brave plum porridge and a roasted pullet," supplemented only by a bought mince pie.

On Christmas morning in parts of the Middle East, people take a type of shortbread called *"kaik"* as a gift to the friends and neighbors they visit. It is eaten with a traditional drink called *"shortbat."*

In Zimbabwe a Christmas feast is sometimes shared by members of a church after the morning service. It often consists of porridge, bread, jam, tea, and sugar, and sometimes roast ox or goat.

If you are in a hot climate at Christmas, why not try a new Australian tradition? Many people in Australia now celebrate with a barbecue or a picnic on the beach because seafood and cold meats are much more suited to the weather than a huge roast turkey dinner.

Jamaicans usually have a big feast at Christmas, which often includes rice and gungo beans, chicken, oxtail, curried goat, and fresh fruit. Their preferred Christmas drink is *"sorrel,"* a delicious concoction made from dried sorrel sepals, cinnamon, cloves, sugar, orange peel, and rum.

All you that to feasting and mirth are inclined,
Come, here is good news for to pleasure your mind,
Old Christmas is come for to keep open house,
He scorns to be guilty of starving a mouse:
Then come, boys, and welcome for diet the chief,
Plum-pudding, goose, capon, minced pies and roast beef.

Traditional poem

Henry VIII's plum pies measured 9 feet long, weighed 165 pounds, and had to be wheeled to the table on a huge cart! They each contained 8 different kinds of meat, 2 bushels of flour, and 24 pounds of butter.

Why get tied to a turkey at Christmas? Samuel Pepys's diary also shows us that during the 1660s his Christmas dinners included a "shoulder of mutton," and in 1666 "some good ribs of beef roasted and mince pies...and plenty of good wine."

What are brown and creep around the house?
Mince spies!

Turn food into a feast by garnishing your platters and table with ivy leaves and flowers, floating candles, and pine cones.

Mince pie has always been an important feature of Christmas festivities in England. The Puritans called it "superstitious" pie in protest against what they believed was a pagan way to celebrate a holy feast.

Contrary to what you would expect, English mincemeat pies are not made with meat at all. They are actually filled with a mixture of raisins, suet, apples, currants, sugar, candied citrus peels, and cinnamon.

It is quite simple to make your own mince pies, but you may prefer just to make your own pie crusts and to buy a jar of pre-made mincemeat, which is widely available now.

For dramatic effect, place a candle in the center of an artichoke, red cabbage, or bunch of asparagus. A platter of small mince pies liberally sprinkled with powdered sugar, a candle, a few pine twigs, and a pine cone or two conjures up images of snow-covered mountain slopes.

Good bread and good drink, a good fire in the hall,
Brawn, pudding, and souse, and good mustard withal.
Beef, mutton, and pork, and good pies of the best,
Pig, veal, goose, and capon, and turkey well drest,
Cheese, apples and nuts, and good carols to hear,
As then in the country is counted good cheer.

Thomas Tusser

Why always stick to the usual sage and onion stuffing? This Christmas, try making your own simple, but delicious, lemon, parsley, and thyme stuffing instead.

Stuffing should not be soggy. For best results, make it fairly loose and crumbly, but firm enough to hold its shape.

Court cooks in the Victorian era sometimes made culinary tributes based on the song "The Twelve Days of Christmas" and sent baskets stuffed with exotic food to famous gastronomes. For example, a "partridge in a pear tree" would come to the table as plump little roasted birds, spiced and garnished with fruit.

"Two turtle doves" were easy—most private households had some form of domestic dovecot that could provide them with pigeons all year round.

"Three French hens" would have been an ample feast because these birds were fattened on a diet of raisins, currants, milk, breadcrumbs, and suet until their legs couldn't carry them!

"Four calling birds" would have been songbirds—blackbirds and thrushes were regularly eaten, particularly in pies. Imagine a line of sparrows, larks, thrushes, and other songbirds threaded onto a skewer roasting in front of an open fire.

"Six geese a-laying" was easy, too. Goose was the accepted, traditional Christmas fare. These would have been served on a platter, surrounded by deviled goose and hen's eggs. Goose, like duck, is a fatty bird without much meat, so it's important to cook enough to go round.

"Seven swans a-swimming" would be too much for most tables, but in England, with the River Thames playing host to thousands of swans, swan used to be on the Christmas menu just as regularly as duck or goose.

Other traditional, but unusual, delicacies included cormorants, squirrels, herons, bears, and wild boar. Roasted, stewed, or casseroled, each provided a flavorsome addition to the seasonal feast. Wild boar is coming back into fashion now and it actually tastes quite good.

Bob said he didn't believe there ever was such a goose cooked. Its tenderness and flavour, size and cheapness, were the themes of universal admiration. Eked out by apple sauce and mashed potatoes, it was a sufficient dinner for the whole family…

Charles Dickens

For those unable to afford a goose, there was always "mock-goose," which contained no goose at all. Instead, it was an ox-heart stuffed with sage and onions.

A typical Victorian Christmas dinner menu would consist of: raw oysters, bouillon, fried smelts with tartare sauce, potatoes, sweetbread pâtés, peas, roast turkey with cranberry sauce, Roman punch, quail with truffles, rice croquettes, Parisian salad, crackers and cheese, "Nesselrode pudding," fancy cakes, fruit, and coffee.

In medieval days, before changes in hunting laws, wild game played a huge part in the winter and Christmas diet of all classes.

Stuffing was invented to do two things: maintain the moisture and flavor of game and make the food go further.

Today people often think of stuffing as a pre-packaged sage mix, whereas medieval palates were tantalized with the rich flavors and textures of saffron, oysters, chestnuts, cinnamon, oranges, lemons, prunes, port, cloves, and anchovies mixed together with grated bread and suet.

Cranberries are not the only soft fruits that make excellent sauces to serve with turkey and game at Christmas. Try the traditional rowanberries, bilberries, and redcurrants, if you can find them. Each provides a bitter-sweet accompaniment to the meal.

Apples, onions, turnips, and red cabbage are all good to cook with Christmas poultry and game.

Venison, rabbit, and pigeons make superb casseroles or game pies to eat with a good mustard and a bottle of claret on St. Stephen's Day.

In Victorian times turkeys were roasted beside long strings of succulent sausages. Of course, the best way to keep your turkey moist is to cook it breast down!

Try roasting a platter of pheasant, grouse, partridge, and mallard and serving it for Christmas Eve or the day after Christmas. Look for these birds on the Internet if you don't live near a specialty butcher's.

The best thing to put
into any Christmas
dinner is your teeth!

Voices:
For &
Against

Christmas with its joys and raptures passes all too quickly. Perhaps this is a reason why some people are reluctant to go into it in the first place.

"A merry Christmas, Uncle! God save you!"
cried a cheerful voice.
"Bah!" said Scrooge. "Humbug!"

Charles Dickens

Christmas waves a magic
wand over this world, and
behold, everything is softer
and more beautiful.

Norman Vincent Peale

Mirth is like a flash of lightning that breaks through a gloom of clouds and glitters for a moment; cheerfulness keeps up a kind of daylight in the mind and fills it with a steady and perpetual serenity.

Joseph Addison

Everyone counts the days to Christmas and nobody looks back at how long ago the last one was. Christmas is something we eagerly anticipate.

At Christmas the entire world is united in a conspiracy— a conspiracy of love.

The cure, of course is to simply ignore it. You have to put up with about four years of disgrace when you receive Christmas cards and do not send them, but after that you know that the people who send you Christmas cards are doing it to please you and that they don't expect a reply.

Quentin Crisp

Some seem determined to dislike Christmas because the spiritual meaning of the feast is overshadowed these days by commercialism and more material worship.

Christmas is not a date. It is a state of mind.

Mary Ellen Chase

What is Christmas to you? A season of frantic last-minute shopping, hours spent cooking, mile after mile of sticky tape and Christmas paper, and handmade knitted sweaters? Why?

The prospect of Christmas appals me.

Evelyn Waugh

The purpose and cause of the incarnation was that He might illuminate the world by His wisdom and excite it to the love of Himself.

Peter Abelard

Christmas is a time for love, joy, and peace: three things we all wish to experience. Nobody can possibly look forward to Christmas when they fear and dread what it is going to be like.

The Grinch: "That's what it's always been about! Gifts, gifts, gifts…. Look, I don't wanna make waves, but this whole Christmas season is stupid, stupid, stupid!"

Jim Carrey as The Grinch in
How the Grinch Stole Christmas (2000)

Christmas is here:
Winds whistle shrill,
Icy and chill.
Little care we;
Little we fear
Weather without,
Sheltered about
The Mahogany Tree.

William Makepeace Thackeray

When Christmas has been welcomed into our heart, it remains with us for evermore.

We are perhaps less affected by the seasons than our agricultural forebears, but somehow remain affiliated with the presumption that real old-fashioned Christmases should be white with snow.

How many old recollections, and how many dormant sympathies, does Christmas time awaken!

Charles Dickens

Christmas is a season to cherish peace and good will.

Christmas is the season for kindling the fire of hospitality in the hall, the genial flame of charity in the heart.

Washington Irving

Christmas is the joy of brightening other lives.

Midnight, and the clock strikes. It is Christmas Day, the werewolves' birthday, the door of the solstice still wide enough open to let them all slink through.

Angela Carter

Unless we make Christmas an occasion to share our blessings, all the snow in Alaska won't make it "white."

Bing Crosby

Come worship the King,
That little dear thing,
Asleep on His Mother's soft breast.
Ye bright stars, bow down,
Weave for Him a crown,
Christ Jesus by angels confessed.

G. A. Studdert Kennedy

Christmas answers our fundamental
human desire to down tools, cease
work, and have cause to rejoice in the
bleak midwinter.

The merry family gatherings—
The old, the very young;
The strangely lovely way they
Harmonize in carols sung.

For Christmas is tradition time—
Traditions that recall
The precious memories down the years,
The sameness of them all.

Helen Lowrie Marshall

A Christmas heart thinks of others first.

Call a truce, then, to our labours—let us feast with friends and neighbours, and be merry as the custom of our caste; for if "faint and forced the laughter," and if sadness follow after, we are richer by one mocking Christmas past.

Rudyard Kipling

The nicest wrapping of all is, without doubt, the loving family who are wrapped up in each other.

I heard the bells on Christmas Day
Their old, familiar carols play,
And wild and sweet the words repeat
Of peace on earth, good-will to men!
Henry Wadsworth Longfellow

The secret is to learn how to turn a day that can be stressful into one of peace, love, and goodwill toward others.

This the month, and this the happy morn,
Wherein the Son of Heaven's Eternal King,
Of wedded maid and virgin mother born,
Our great redemption from above did bring;

John Milton

Christmas...is not an eternal event at all, but a piece of one's home that one carries in one's heart...

Freya Stark

In the days before Christmas, city streets echo to the sounds of anguished parents in frantic, last-minute, panicked searches for the latest "in" toys, which have inevitably sold out by the first week of Advent.

Christmas is a time for generosity.

A three-year-old child is a being who gets almost as much fun out of a fifty-six dollar set of swings as it does out of finding a small green worm.

Bill Vaughan

Church pews long empty are now dusted, ready for the arrival of the seasonal throng eager to make their peace and to reconnect with the true spirit of Christmas.

Whatever else be lost among the years,
Let us keep Christmas still a shining thing:
Whatever doubts assail us, or what fears,
Let us hold close one day, remembering
Its poignant meaning for the hearts of men.
Let us get back our childlike faith again.

Grace Noll Crowell

Time was with most of us, when Christmas Day, encircling all our limited world like a magic ring, left nothing out for us to miss or seek; bound together all our home enjoyments, affections, and hopes; grouped everything and everyone round the Christmas fire, and made the little picture shining in our bright young eyes, complete.

Charles Dickens

Let your Christmas wish be that every cup may overflow with blessings.

Telephone calls to distant friends, bequests to good causes, we're different now— caring and sharing is now at the forefront of our minds.

Christmas cannot be perfect where it is fueled by greed.

The more you spend in blessing,
The poor and lonely and sad,
The more of your heart's possessing,
Returns to you glad.

John Greenleaf Whittier

As night falls on Christmas
Eve, a spell is woven,
childhood memories spring
to mind, and the world takes
on new meaning.

The rooms were very still while the pages were softly turned and the winter sunshine crept in to touch the bright heads and serious faces with a Christmas greeting.

Louisa May Alcott

Electronic whirring, buzzing, and blips
Fill the rooms.
Each unwrapped gizmo and gadget,
Thrillingly non-straightforward!

Few young hearts today, were you to choose
to misinform them, would ever believe that
Santa had not been there a few hours earlier.

**This day is more than a date; it is a
state of mind, it is a way of being.**

I once bought my kids a set of batteries
for Christmas with a note on it saying,
toys not included.

Bernard Manning

Heap on the wood!—the wind is chill;
But let it whistle as it will,
We'll keep our Christmas merry still.

Sir Walter Scott

Outside the weather may do its worst
Rain, snow, hail, or frost.
Inside, friends and family
Are safe in the comfort of each other's company
And warmed by merrymaking.

Merry Christmas,
Nearly Everybody!

Ogden Nash

At Christmas play and make good cheer,
For Christmas comes but once a year.

Thomas Tusser

One can close off one's senses to many things in life, but to choose to close them to Christmas is to close off oneself from joy.

Break forth, O beauteous heavenly light,
And usher in the morning;
O shepherds, shrink not with afright,
But hear the angel's warning.
This Child, now weak in infancy,
Our confidence and joy shall be,
The power of Satan breaking,
Our peace eternal making.

Johann Rist

Roses are reddish
Violets are bluish
If it weren't for Christmas
We'd all be Jewish.

Benny Hill

When you light a Christmas fire in your hearth, feel its Christmas warmth in your heart.

The only real blind person at Christmas time is he who has not Christmas in his heart.

Helen Keller

Christmas is like a grand opera tour. It takes months in the preparation, a few hours to perform, then hits the road and disappears for another year.

We consider Christmas as the encounter, the great encounter, the historical encounter, the decisive encounter, between God and mankind. He who has faith knows this truly; let him rejoice.

Pope Paul VI

Let no pleasure tempt thee, no profit allure thee, no persuasion move thee, to do anything which thou knowest to be evil; so shalt thou always live jollity; for a good conscience is a continual Christmas.

Benjamin Franklin

It is often said that if Christmas did not exist, it would be necessary to invent it.

At Christmas I no more desire a rose

Than wish a snow in May's new fangled mirth;

But like of each thing that in season grows.

William Shakespeare

Christmas is love in action.

When one becomes firmly resolved
to celebrate Christmas, nothing that
chance, destiny, or fate can throw in
your way can loosen that.

**Bless us Lord, this Christmas, with quietness of mind;
Teach us to be patient and always to be kind.**
Helen Steiner Rice

It is sad perhaps that, for most
of us, Christmas is the only
time of the year when we dare
reveal our true selves.

With so many beliefs, so many paths, the world needs only one thing from each of us to unite us all at Christmas—a simple act of kindness.

May all my enemies go to hell, Noel, Noel, Noel, Noel.

Hilaire Belloc

The secret is not to look at Christmas as a time to be dreaded but to enter into the season willingly and wholeheartedly.

And numerous indeed are the hearts to which Christmas brings a brief season of happiness and enjoyment. How many families, whose members have been dispersed and scattered far and wide, in the restless struggles of life, are then reunited, and meet once again in that happy state of companionship and mutual goodwill…

Charles Dickens

Never expect too much of Christmas Day. You cannot force it to go in any particular direction. It will follow the ebb and flow of the humanity and kindliness that you and those gathered with you bring to it.

A man is at his finest towards the finish
  of the year;
He is almost what he should be when
  the Christmas season's here;
Then he's thinking more of others than
  he's thought the months before,
And the laughter of his children is a joy
  worth toiling for.

Edgar Guest

The paths to Christmas lead to peace.

The joy of Christmas is passed from heart to heart.

Glory to God in highest heaven,
Who unto man His Son hath given;
While angels sing with tender mirth,
A glad new year to all the earth.

Martin Luther

There has been only one real Christmas. We tend to forget that the rest have been anniversaries.

Christmas in Bethlehem. The ancient dream: a cold, clear night made brilliant by a glorious star, the smell of incense, shepherds and wise men falling to their knees in adoration of the sweet baby, the incarnation of perfect love.

Lucinda Franks

Remember, it is the same wind that drives us all. No matter what direction you approach Christmas from, it's the way you set your sails that determines how you get through it.

Green groweth the holly,
So doth the ivy.
Though winter blasts blow never so high,
Green groweth the holly.

Henry VIII

A woman spent all Christmas Day in a telephone box without ringing anyone. If someone comes to phone, she leaves the box, then resumes her place afterwards. No one calls her either, but from a window in the street, someone watched her all day, no doubt since they had nothing better to do. The Christmas syndrome.

Jean Baudrillard

Who of us wants to go to our grave and have it said by those we leave behind, "here was a person who had no idea of how to keep Christmas"?

Now the flames of the fire glow warm and inviting,
Now the hospitable glow of charity warms the heart.

No matter how old the world grows, Christmas remains young and vibrant—and so too do those who celebrate it.

A merry Christmas to everybody! A happy New Year to all the world!

Charles Dickens

Lou Lou Who: "You can't hurt Christmas, Mr. Mayor, because it isn't about the gifts or the contest or the fairy lights…. I don't need anything more for Christmas than this right here: my family."

Bill Irwin as Lou Lou Who in
How the Grinch Stole Christmas (2000)

Those who love Christmas are themselves loved.

The Church does not superstitiously observe days, merely as days, but as memorials of important facts. Christmas might be kept as well upon one day of the year as another; but there should be a stated day for commemorating the birth of our Saviour, because there is danger that what may be done on any day, will be neglected.

Samuel Johnson

Christmas is a voyage we all go on together. Only, inevitably, there are those who are determined to rock the boat.

Where is this stupendous stranger?
Prophets, shepherds, kings, advise;
Lead me to my Master's manger,
Show me where my Saviour lies.

Christopher Smart

This little Babe, so few days old,
Is come to rifle Satan's fold;
All hell doth at his presence quake,
Though he himself for cold do shake;
For in this weak unarmed wise
The gates of hell he will surprise.

Robert Southwell

That the Creator himself comes to us and becomes our ransom—this is the reason for our rejoicing.

Martin Luther

Love came down at Christmas,
Love all lovely, Love Divine;
Love was born at Christmas;
Star and angels gave the sign.

Christina Rossettii

Unto us a Son is given!
He has come from God's own heaven,
Bringing with Him, from above,
Holy peace and holy love.

Horatius Bonar

If only we could preserve the Christmas spirit and serve small portions of it throughout the year.

While we celebrate Christmas Day in December, the spirit of Christmas remains with us throughout the year in all that we do and say.

Christmas remains a time to forget about the long dark days and celebrate with friends and family.

Traditions &
Celebrations
From Around
the World

December arrives. In England it's the hoar-frost month; in old Dutch it's *"Winter-maand"* or winter-month; in old Saxon, *"Mid-winter-monath;"* while Christian Saxons referred to it as *"Se ura geóla"* or the anti-Yule. But no matter how it's known, it's the time to look forward to celebrating Christmas.

Worldwide, it's traditional to give good children shoes or stockings filled with tangerines, nuts, chocolates, and small gifts, while misbehaving children can look forward to anything from lumps of coal and old potatoes to a shovel-load of manure!

A pessimistic "good" child might fret and worry about damaging a new toy on Christmas morning, while an optimistic "bad" child might see the manure and believe that they've been given a pony!

Each of us has our own tradition for opening gifts. Some prefer Christmas Eve while others do it early on Christmas morning.

French nuns may have begun a custom that spread throughout Europe when they began leaving treats of apples, oranges, nuts, cookies, and candies on the eve of St. Nicholas's Day for the children of poor families.

"Buon Natale" and *"Felice Anno Nuovo"* from Italy, where on 6 January, Epiphany, children who have been good receive *"la calza,"* a colorful stocking full of sweets and the bad ones receive stockings filled with *"il carbone,"* which is a coal-like substance made of black sugar.

In Germany naughty children are terrified by a seasonal character called Frau Bertha! She is a huge woman with extremely large feet and a nose of iron, who steals into nurseries and rocks infants to sleep.

There is a figure similar to Santa Claus among the Lapps known as "The Yule Swain." However, he is different in that he is about 11 feet tall, and instead of a sleigh, he rides on a goat and makes visits between St. Thomas's Day and Christmas Eve.

It is well-known in the Swedish countryside that from cock crow to daybreak on Christmas morning the trolls will roam.

"Kala Christougena" from Greece, where on 1 January, St. Basil, the Greek version of Father Christmas, expects a slice of New Year sponge cake laid out for him in return for the gifts he delivers. A silver coin is traditionally hidden in the cake for one lucky child to find.

In Portugal children place their shoes by the fireplace—hoping they will be filled with gifts—but they ask the infant Jesus for their gifts, not Santa Claus.

The Scandinavians wish everyone *"Glaedelig Jul"* and start celebrating the holiday season as early as 13 December, St. Lucia's Day, when the eldest daughter, dressed in white, wears a wreath crown that has seven lit candles on it. Moving carefully, she serves coffee and homemade cakes to her family.

On Christmas Eve in 1492, Christopher Columbus's ship was wrecked on a coral reef near the island that we know today as Haiti. The island's ruler helped Columbus and spent Christmas Day dining with him. A small fortress now stands on the site where the celebration took place. It is called *"La Navidad"* or the Nativity.

There is a legend still observed in some parts of the world that when you blow out the candles on Christmas Eve, you should watch the direction that the smoke takes. If it moves toward the window, the harvest will be good and if it moves toward the stove, there will be a marriage.

The Scandinavians used to believe that if enemies met under the mistletoe they would forgive each other and embrace—hence the tradition of kissing under the mistletoe.

In some parts of Europe, when boys kiss girls under the mistletoe they picked one berry for each kiss. When the berries ran out, the kissing had to stop!

In some parts of Luxembourg, a donkey carries the toys and sweets and St. Nicholas is accompanied by a figure called *"Housécker"* (Black Peter or Père Fouettard) who brings a bag of switches.

St. Nicholas, known as *"Klees'chen,"* comes to Luxembourg to check and see if the children deserve any presents. At the town hall, a crowd of happy, excited children beg in verse for bonbons. St. Nicholas gives each child a bag filled with apples, cakes, and sweets.

Throughout the world today you can find Christmas tree decorations that include painted eggshells, cookies, gingerbread, nuts, and candies.

In France the Twelfth Night is still celebrated. A charm is baked in a cake and whoever finds it becomes King or Queen for the day.

Nuremberg in Bavaria was the first place to produce metal and foil ornaments for Christmas trees. They exported them worldwide in designs such as miniature musical instruments, butterflies, stars, and icicles.

Dresden and Leipzig, in Germany, were famous producers of embossed paper and cardboard ornaments known as "Dresdens," and also made angel's hair.

The creation of delicate blown-glass ornaments began in the Thuringian mountains and Lauscha in Eastern Germany.

The oddest German decorations are glass pickle ornaments. The tradition is that parents would hide the pickle and on Christmas morning the children would hunt for it. The lucky child who found it hung it on the tree and not only got to be the first to open a present, but also had a special extra treat from St. Nicholas.

Passed from generation to generation, the box of family Christmas tree ornaments is the most likely thing to bring back treasured memories of Christmases past.

The bell ornament represents the joy of the season. It is legend that bells tolled when Jesus was born and in many countries they still ring out to welcome him at Christmas.

In Greek the letter "X" is a symbol for Christ, which is why Christmas is often shortened to "XMAS."

When you visit during the Christmas season in many places, it's a tradition to give your host or hostess a tree ornament that's shaped like a coffee pot. Because it represents good hospitality, it shows your appreciation.

Little fruit basket ornaments signify the hope of plenty in the year to come and also a charitable disposition.

Blown-glass rabbit ornaments represent the fragility of man in nature and his belief in God's mercy. Hang them with a wish for protection, guidance, and love.

The fish is a traditional German Christmas ornament and is a symbol of Christianity.

Many homes have a bird or little robin hung on their tree to bring happiness and joy to the family.

In many places it's a tradition to hide a bird's nest somewhere in the Christmas tree. It brings good luck to the person who spots it.

Ladybug ornaments are hung as thanks and for good luck. This legend arose at a time when insects threatened to ruin the crops and only after the farmers prayed to Holy Mary did legions of ladybugs arrive and eat all the pests. That's why they were named after "Our Lady."

Wooden or blown-glass mushrooms are hung as ornaments to represent the mysteries of nature— an ornament of two mushrooms stuck together is a symbol of good luck at Christmas.

A star is often hung or placed on the top of the Christmas tree as a sign of faith and guidance and to remind everyone of the star of Bethlehem that guided the Magi.

No tree is complete without the addition of angels, which signify God's messengers, all that is pure, love, and peace on earth.

Stemming from the time when Christmas trees were decorated with actual fruit, blown glass and wooden carved apples have been hung in many countries as a sign to avoid temptation.

In England people hung acorns in many woodland areas to represent the baby Jesus and how something so small could, like the oak, grow into something so mighty.

Pine cones as Christmas decorations are believed to celebrate fertility and motherhood.

Hanging fairy hair or angel's hair on the Christmas tree comes from a Romanian folk tale of a poor family who could not afford to decorate the tree they cut in the forest. The night before Christmas, a spider spun an intricate and beautiful glistening web around the tree that they discovered on Christmas morning.

General George Washington crossed the Delaware River on Christmas Eve of 1776, knowing that British soldiers would be celebrating the holiday rather than keeping a watchful eye.

Christmas trees are derived from the legend of St. Boniface, who cut down a mighty oak that pagans had been using as a roof under which they made sacrifices. A young fir sapling appeared in its place and was adopted as a sign of God's everlasting love.

In Latvia around 1510 a fir tree was decorated with roses because they were associated with the Virgin Mary.

In 1605, a Christmas tree in Strasbourg was brought indoors and decorated with paper roses, wafers, nuts, lighted candles, and sweets.

The day to prepare your traditional Advent wreath is 30 November. It is also St. Andrew's Day—the day on which we should celebrate Andrew, who was one of the first four disciples and is the patron saint of the Order of the Golden Fleece.

Christmas at the Elizabethan court included richly costumed masquerades, colorful pageants, and great feasts of roasted ox, wild boar, and swan. It's believed that Shakespeare wrote *Twelfth Night* to be performed at the Christmas 1601 court festivities.

In Egypt the Coptic Church celebrates Christmas on 7 December. Advent is traditionally observed for forty days before this, which means people are expected to fast and cannot eat meat, poultry, or dairy products.

Poinsettias are very popular plants at Christmas. Their red leaves symbolize the blood of Christ, their white leaves his purity, and their shape the star of Bethlehem.

Ukrainians prepare a traditional twelve-course meal. A family's youngest child watches through the window for the evening star to appear, a signal that the feast can begin.

In Greece many people believe in *"kallikantzeri,"* goblins that appear and cause mischief during the Twelve Days of Christmas.

A manger scene is the primary decoration in most southern European, Central American, and South American nations.

St. Francis of Assisi created the first living nativity in 1224 to help explain the birth of Jesus to his followers because many were illiterate or couldn't understand Latin, so the nativity was a way for them to appreciate the Christmas story.

St. Francis wanted to show people what the first Christmas must have been like on that night in Bethlehem, so he set up a nativity scene with live animals and a manger filled with hay. People from his village played the parts to make it seem real.

The turkey was imported to France by the Jesuits and is still known in some French dialects as a "Jesuite."

In some parts of France, children place shoes by the fire and wake up on Christmas Day to find them filled with gifts from *"Le Père Noël."* They discover nuts, fruit, and small toys hanging on their tree.

The French Christmas revolves around the children and their presents, and many adults wait until New Year's Eve to open their gifts.

Le Père Noël has a helper known as *"Le Père Fouettard"* (Father Spanker) whose task is to decide whether children have been good or bad that year and "reward" bad children with a spanking!

The first mention of a candle being used at Christmas time is from the Middle Ages—a large candle was used to represent the star of Bethlehem.

On Christmas Eve in Bethlehem, residents and pilgrims crowd the Church of the Nativity for a glimpse of the dramatic procession of horsemen. They are followed by the solitary horseman who carries a cross on a black steed, followed in turn by the clergy who solemnly move through the doors to place an ancient effigy of the Christ Child in the church.

In the Church of the Nativity in Bethlehem, a deep, winding staircase leads to a grotto where pilgrims can find a silver star marking what is said to be the place where Jesus was born.

In Poland, when St. Nicholas appears, the eager children cry, "He has come! He has come!" and he watches with a twinkle in his eye as the children recite their catechism and prayers.

St. Nicholas, called *"Sw. Mikolaj"* in Poland, distributes holy pictures, apples or oranges, and *"pierniki,"* which are saint cookies made with honey and spices.

A "Christingle" is a decorated orange with a candle in it. The name means "Christ Light" and it is a symbol of the light of Jesus coming into the world. The first Christingles were given to German children by a bishop in 1747. Children in Britain often make them to raise money for charity and they have their own special Christingle services.

The Christingle orange represents the world, the red ribbon around it is the blood of Christ, the fruits symbolize God's creation, and the candle represents Jesus as Light of the World.

To make your own Christingle, take an orange and cut a small cross in the top. Cover the cross with a square of aluminum foil and then firmly push a candle through the foil into the orange. Then fasten a length of red ribbon around the middle of the orange. Next, feed raisins, sultanas, cherries or small soft sweets onto four cocktail sticks. Insert these into the orange around the base of the candle and above the ribbon.

Francis Kipps Spencer made the first "Chrismons" in Virginia. They are hung in churches and on Christmas trees to remind people that they are celebrating Jesus's birthday. They are traditionally white and gold and are often made from paper or fabric, but they can feature any Christian symbol or monogram.

German Father Christmas—*"Der Weihnachtsmann"*—brings presents in the late afternoon of Christmas Eve, after people have been to a church meeting. The presents are found under the Christmas tree. One person in the family rings a bell and calls everyone to come to the room.

In Austria St. Nicholas arrives on 6 December and brings presents only to good children who leave him hay and brandy.

If you are in Greece, you should burn your old shoes during the Christmas season to prevent falling into misfortunes in the coming year.

In Belgium people celebrate on Christmas Eve with a special feast called *"le réveillon de Noël."*

Santa Claus is known in Belgium by his traditional name, St. Nicholas, and he brings gifts to children on 6 December. Families also give one another presents at Christmas. They are left under the tree or in stockings near the fireplace, to be found in the morning.

Traditionally, St. Nicholas quizzed Czech children on the Bible. The Recording Angel wrote each child's record in a large book and, while the children sang to the saint, the Devil rattled his chains and threatened to carry the bad children off.

In Prague there is a carnival where prizes are given for the best masks. In the early evening of 6 December, St. Nicholas visits children at home with his entourage of the Devil and an angel.

In the Czech Republic angels lower St. Nicholas—*"Svaty Mikulá"*—down from heaven on a heavy golden cord. He is accompanied by a devil who takes bad children away and an angel who pleads on their behalf.

In Brazil many Christmas customs are similar to those in America or Britain. People who can afford to eat turkey, ham, rice, salad, pork, and fresh and dried fruits, often with beer, while people with little money celebrate with chicken and rice.

Finnish people clean their houses to prepare for the three holy days of Christmas—Christmas Eve, Christmas Day, and Boxing Day. Cemeteries are very beautiful at Christmas time, because many families place candles on family graves.

In Holland children leave their shoes beside the hearth with hay and carrots for the reindeer. The next morning, the hay has been replaced with pink sweets filled with chocolate.

Children in Finland receive their presents on Christmas Eve—usually from a family member dressed as Father Christmas.

Finnish people believe that Father Christmas lives in Korvatunturi, a part of Finland north of the Arctic Circle. People from all over the world send letters to Santa Claus in Finland.

But the people of Greenland contend that Father Christmas lives in Greenland!

One tradition in Brazil is to create a nativity scene. This is called a *"Presépio,"* which comes from the Hebrew word for the bed of straw upon which the infant Jesus slept in Bethlehem. A Franciscan friar made the first *Presépio* in the seventeenth century and they are now set up in churches, stores, and homes.

Papai Noel brings gifts from his home in Greenland to children in Brazil. Legends say that he wears silk clothing because of the hot weather.

Devout Catholics in Brazil often attend Midnight Mass on Christmas Eve. It is also known as *"Missa do Galo"* because the rooster, *"galo,"* announces the coming of Christmas morning when the mass finishes at around 1:00AM.

On Belgian St. Nicholas's Eve, children put their shoes or small baskets at the hearth with carrots, turnips, and a sugar lump for the saint's horse. They believe that St. Nicholas rides on horseback over the rooftops, dropping his gifts down the chimneys.

In the East Flanders town of Sint-Niklaas, the saint brings his treats the weekend before 6 December. The following Monday is a school holiday, which gives children a three-day weekend to play with their new toys.

In French-speaking Wallonia St. Nicholas comes accompanied by a donkey and Père Fouettard, as he does in France. Other parts of Germany celebrate in much the same way as people do in Germany.

In Kenya missionaries often provide Christmas dinners in poor areas and decorate churches with balloons, ribbons, and flowers.

St. Nicholas's Day is a very special day in the village of St. Nikola an der Donau on the River Danube. Following a service in the church, a long procession goes down to the riverbanks and the children watch the boats in the river. Suddenly all the boat sirens sound at once because the boat bringing St. Nicholas arrives.

In Zimbabwe those who celebrate Christmas, *"Kisimusi,"* often decorate fir trees on Christmas Eve with colorful handmade ornaments. Gifts are placed under the tree and a family member distributes them.

Germans love to decorate their houses at Christmas. They often have an *"Adventskranz,"* a wreath of leaves with four candles. On each Sunday of Advent, they light another candle on it. Most homes also have little wooden cribs, or small model nativity scenes.

The first official Christmas in Australia was celebrated in 1788 at Sydney Cove. The Governor and his officers had a traditional Christmas meal, but the convicts were given only their normal rations of bread!

In France statues and paintings often portray the miracle of St. Nicholas bringing three children in a salt barrel back to life after they had been murdered by an evil butcher.

In Australia and New Zealand Christmas falls in the middle of summer and because it is so warm, flowers are often the main decorations. The Christmas bush plant with its small red-flowered leaves is a popular choice.

In Melbourne, Australia, in 1937, thousands of people came together to sing Christmas songs. This "Carols by Candlelight" celebration has become a tradition. Today it is broadcast across the world.

Canada is such a multicultural country that its traditions come from all over the world. In Nova Scotia Scottish customs and songs are popular and masked "mummers" may be seen ringing bells in the streets at Christmas time.

In some Canadian provinces the Eskimos celebrate a winter festival called *"Sinck tuck."* They give presents and have family meals and parties, just as others do at Christmas.

Although very few people in Japan believe in Christ, some still like to decorate their homes and give gifts at Christmas. Many Japanese Christians spend the festive season doing good deeds for others who may be sick, poor, or elderly.

In Japan a priest called "Hoteiosha" has a similar role to Santa Claus—leaving presents for well-behaved children.

Christmas is a very special time for Jamaicans and they add a tropical flavor to the festivities. In some areas they have a "Jonkanoo" celebration at Christmas. This tradition was brought over from Africa and includes a festive parade.

In France Christmas trees are often decorated with red ribbons and white wax candles.

The Christmas meal in France is an important family gathering with excellent meat and the finest wine.

Austrian children leave shoes for St. Nicholas on the windowsill or outside their bedroom doors. In the morning they find that the saint has filled good children's shoes with oranges, apples, nuts, sweets, and small toys.

Austrian *"Christkindlmarkts"* open before St. Nicholas's Day. These markets sell delightful St. Nicholas delicacies—chocolates, marzipan, decorated cookies, even bread shaped like the good saint. The treats can be very small—you can find treats such as a single wrapped chocolate turned into a handmade little Bishop Nicholas.

Nutcrackers were very popular Christmas gifts with Germans who coined the phrase, "God gives the nuts, but we have to crack them ourselves."

In Switzerland, France, Germany, and England during the sixteenth and seventeenth centuries, nutcrackers were given as keepsakes because they were believed to bring good luck and to guard against evil spirits.

In Germany near the Bohemian border, most villagers worked in the mines, but carved wooden nutcrackers during the long winter months. The nutcrackers were usually designed to resemble bosses, kings, soldiers and rulers, and people liked the idea of these powerful figures being placed at their service to crack nuts for them.

In Latvia, Father Christmas brings presents on each of the 12 days of Christmas, starting on Christmas Eve. Usually the presents are put under the Christmas tree.

The special Christmas Day meal in Latvia is brown peas with bacon, sauce, small pies, cabbage, and sausage.

In Portugal, Father Christmas brings presents to children on Christmas Eve, leaving them under the Christmas tree or in shoes by the fireplace.

A special meal is eaten at midnight on Christmas Eve in Portugal and it usually consists of salted dry cod-fish with boiled potatoes.

In Russia during the days of the Soviet Union, Christmas was not celebrated much, but New Year was an important time when "Father Frost" brought presents to children.

Christmas is now openly celebrated by some people in Russia on 25 December, but most people celebrate on 7 January, because the Russian Orthodox church uses the old Julian calendar for religious celebration days.

St. Nicholas is honored throughout Austria. It is said that God rewarded Nicholas's generosity by allowing him to return to earth each year to bring gifts to all the good children.

In several European countries St. Nicholas traditionally comes on his feast day, a special holiday that is not part of the Christmas celebrations. In some countries he comes on St. Nicholas's Eve, 5 December, but in others, on the day itself, 6 December.

In Austria a strange and frightening creature, "Krampus," is traditionally with St. Nicholas. This devil figure, often in chains, is dressed in fur with a scary mask and a long red tongue. Krampus carries a wooden stick to threaten children who misbehave, but St. Nicholas never lets Krampus harm anyone.

In Austria St. Nicholas comes dressed as a bishop with flowing robes and a mitre. He carries a big book and a bishop's crozier. Angels, who sometimes accompany him, write children's good and bad deeds in this book all through the year.

The famous Christmas song "Jingle Bells" was composed in 1857 by James Pierpont. However, it was actually written for Thanksgiving, not Christmas.

In some Austrian towns St. Nicholas marches from the church before giving little presents to all the children. St. Nicholas may also visit homes to ask children if they have been naughty or nice and sometimes asks them to recite their prayers.

In Dutch-speaking Flanders, colorful parades greet St. Nicholas with bands and banners picturing the saint. He and his assistants come in November by boat, train, or on horseback to get ready for his feast day.

The Dutch Sinterklaas season is mainly a children's festival because 6 December is a special day for children, rather than for whole families. St. Nicholas visits and asks children if they have done their best during the year, then he checks in his book to see if they are telling the truth.

"Nikulden" is a great Bulgarian winter festival celebrating St. Nicholas, the protector of sailors and fishermen. The fishing season ends on Nikulden when the day's catch is offered to the saint. Fishermen eat the first fish they catch at the shore and then take the rest of the fish home.

In the nineteenth century the British Post Office delivered cards even on Christmas morning.

In Croatia St. Nicholas—"Sveti Nikola"—brings gifts to children on his feast day. This is when most people give gifts. On the eve of St. Nicholas's Day, children polish their boots until they gleam before placing them on a windowsill to wait for the good saint.

St. Nicholas fills good Croatian children's shoes with candy, fruit, and gifts. Krampus accompanies him and leaves golden twigs for naughty children—the worse the behavior, the larger the twig.

Traditionally in Italy, the kind witch *"La Befana"* brings the gifts and sweets. It seems that she followed the Wise Men but got lost and has been wandering ever since, handing out presents to children at Christmas.

In Venice and Mantova Santa Lucia brings the presents, while in some regions it's baby Jesus who bears the gifts. But today most Italians recognize Father Christmas, "Babbo Natal."

Spanish tradition has it that "los Reyes Magos," the Magi, are the ones who bear presents for all the children on the morning of 6 January, repeating the ritual they performed after baby Jesus was born.

In Cataluña there is a surprising addition to the crib: *"el caganer,"* the defecating shepherd. What's more, this extends to a peculiarly shaped local cake, *"la tifa,"* with sugar flies to top it all off.

All Hallows Eve, 31 October, was the traditional time to elect the Lord of Misrule, or the Christmas King, in British towns. He ruled until Candlemas on 2 February.

The Greeks see St. Nicholas thus—his clothes soaked with brine, his beard dripping with seawater, and his face wet with perspiration and seawater from fighting storms to reach sinking ships and save drowning men.

All Greek ships carry an icon of St. Nicholas and sailors light a candle before it and pray for safe passage. To honor his day, small fishing boats are decorated with blue and white lights.

In Austria an old custom for young women wishing to marry was to take one bite of an apple every day from St. Lucia's Day until Christmas Eve. They had to judge the size of each bite carefully to make sure they took the last bite on Christmas Eve. And then, with luck, they would see their future husbands.

In the Roman Catholic Church, the feast in honor of the Holy Family—Jesus, Mary, and Joseph—usually falls on the first Sunday after the Epiphany.

The Holy Family was a popular theme in Renaissance art, probably deriving from the larger theme of the Nativity in medieval representations, with fine examples by Signorelli, Michelangelo, and da Vinci.

In 1647 the Puritan leader Oliver Cromwell banned Christmas festivities in England because he believed that it was immoral to have fun on a holy day. Anyone caught celebrating Christmas was arrested.

In Britain between Christmas and Easter it was traditionally the "mummers" season. Non-religious mummers plays were performed across the country and they dealt with the issues of death and resurrection to reflect the onslaught of winter and the return of the fertile spring.

In Dublin in 1458 a different Yule play was presented each day of Christmas week by tradesmen of the city. However, the clergy believed that the plays were too pagan and that is when they began to present plays such as *The Passion of Our Lord* and the *Martyrdom of the Apostles.*

In the French regions of Alsace, Lorraine, and Brittany, St. Nicholas comes with a little donkey loaded with baskets filled with children's gifts and treats.

Père Fouettard, who follows St. Nicholas in shame, is meant to be the evil butcher. He carries switches to threaten the children, but what they fear most is that he may advise St. Nicholas to pass them by on his gift-giving rounds.

In Switzerland on the eve of St. Nicholas Day, villages around Lake Lucerne glow with the candlelight from a procession of hundreds of enormous, intricately cut, colored-paper bishops' miters known as *"iffelen"* that look like giant stained-glass windows on legs.

The most spectacular parade is in Küssnacht am Rigi, Switzerland. It begins when a cannon fires, signaling to men cracking long whips to pass by. They are then followed by 300 illuminated iffelen headdresses swaying along. Next comes St. Nicholas, accompanied by his torchbearers and the trumpeters, who are followed by hundreds of Klausjäger men swinging cowbells. Proceedings end with 100 or 200 cow horns being repeatedly blown in unison.

Every year in Bari St. Nicholas's statue is taken out to sea for a day. Thousands welcome it with a long, winding, torch-lit procession to a public square where the mayor and other dignitaries greet the statue and address the crowds.

On St. Nicholas's Eve children in Molfetta, Italy, a city on the Adriatic Sea, put a plate on the dining table with a letter asking for gifts and promising to be good in the coming year.

The Dutch Christmas is about giving, for "it is in giving that we receive." Everyone loves trying to surprise other people, to tease, make jokes, and produce rhymes.

Vladimir the Great introduced stories of St. Nicholas to Russia in the eleventh century. There Nicholas became greatly revered as the protector of the weak from the strong, the oppressed from the oppressor, and the poor from the rich.

St. Nicholas is the Russian champion of the disadvantaged. He is known as the "Miracle Worker."

The impressive Italian "San Nicola" festival commemorates the 1087 arrival of St. Nicholas's remains in Italy after Italian sailors spirited the relics away to Bari. A huge basilica was built in honor of the saint.

Children in Stuttgart dress up as St. Nicholas and go from door to door asking for sweets—much like they go trick-or-treating in America.

On Christmas Day in Germany, fish or goose is traditionally cooked for dinner.

The Christmas breakfast in Belgium traditionally features a special sweet bread called *"cougnou"* or *"cougnolle"* that's made in a shape meant to represent baby Jesus.

Swiss children like to make their own iffelen headdresses and stage their own parade with St. Nicholas. Afterward, they eat a traditional treat of sausage and sauerkraut.

In Finland people awake to a breakfast of rice porridge and plum juice. Afterwards, they decorate a spruce tree they have brought into the house.

A traditional Christmas dinner in Finland includes casseroles containing macaroni, rutabaga, carrot, potato, and ham or turkey.

In some countries it is traditional on New Year's Eve to place a silver coin outside the house. If the coin is still there in the morning, the year ahead will be abundant and bountiful.

In Sweden Christmas Eve is the time for celebrating. Everyone eats a traditional special Christmas meal of ham, herring, and brown beans. This is also when families give each other gifts.

America is so multi-cultural that it's not unusual for Americans to sit down to a Christmas meal made up of dishes from a wide range of countries.

Merry Christmas!